CW01083108

Ninja Dual Zone

Air Fryer

Cookbook

101 Delicious Recipes

for Every Day

Juanita Romero

Copyright ©2021 By **Juanita Romero** All rights reserved.

No part of this guide may be reproduced in any form without permission in writing from the publisher except in the case of brief quotations embodied in critical articles or reviews.

Legal & Disclaimer

The information contained in this book and its contents is not designed to replace or take the place of any form of medical or professional advice; and is not meant to replace the need for independent medical, financial, legal or other professional advice or services, as may be required. The content and information in this book has been provided for educational and entertainment purposes only.

The content and information contained in this book has been compiled from sources deemed reliable, and it is accurate to the best of the Author's knowledge, information and belief. However, the Author cannot guarantee its accuracy and validity and cannot be held liable for any errors and/or omissions. Further, changes are periodically made to this book as and when needed. Where appropriate and/or necessary, you must consult a professional (including but not limited to your doctor, attorney, financial advisor or such other professional advisor) before using any of the suggested remedies, techniques, or information in this book.

CONTENTS

POULTRY RECIPES...62

FISH & SEAFOOD RECIPES...77

INTRODUCTION

The air fryer is the latest kitchen appliance to sweep America off its feet. The air fryer promises to offer a healthy alternative to the very popular but deeply unhealthy fried food. Most people do not fry at home – with the exception of fried turkey at Thanksgiving – but nevertheless, the air fryer still offers great versatility. By cooking its food at very high temperatures almost immediately, it saves cooks a good deal of time and makes cooking a snap. Let's learn about the air fryer.

How Air Fryers Work

An air fryer cooks food by circulating hot air around the food through a traditional convection mechanism. The technology behind the air fryer is nothing exceptionally new. It uses the same process as a convection oven. The hot air is created by a very high-speed fan, which allows for a crispy top layer and tender, juicy interiors. The original air fryer was patented by Turbochef Technologies back in 2005, but its audience was hotel chains and other restaurants.

Phillips introduced its version of the air fryer in 2010 and marketed it to home chefs. The air fryer typically includes a round or egg-shaped fry basket that is easy to clean. Most of the fryer baskets are even dishwasher safe.

Is the Air Fryer Really Healthier?

According to Phillips, "the air fryer technology results in French fries that includes up to 80% less fat than traditionally-fried foods." But are these kinds of claims really true? According to studies, the answer is a qualified yes.

Deep fryers use about 50 times as much oil as their air frying counterparts. The electric fryer's main health benefit is that it cuts down on the amount of oil absorbed by the food, limiting the overall fat content. Food that is fried in oil is always unhealthy and has a lot of fat calories. A chicken breast that is fried has about 30 percent more fat than roasted chicken. An air fryer will not necessarily cook chicken healthier than baking it in an oven, but it will produce the crispy skin that people love in fried chicken.

Another benefit of an air fryer is avoiding the bad compounds which develop during the oil frying process. One of the compounds, acrylamide, may be linked to several cancers, including pancreatic, breast and ovarian cancer. The compound is created during high-heat cooking with oil. This compound does not form during the air frying process.

A study of the characteristics of French fries produced by deep fat frying and air frying found that the air fryer potatoes tasted like traditional French fries but with a substantially lower level of fat absorbed in the product. Again, this is due to the small amount of oil used in the air fryer.

However, you should not cook all of your foods in an air fryer, since air fryers still fry food. Fried foods are linked to heart conditions, high blood pressure, diabetes and some cancers. Limiting fried foods and focusing on healthy cooking methods such as roasting, steaming and sauteing are still best for daily cooking.

Breakfast And Brunch Recipes

Baked Eggs

Servings: 4
Cooking Time: 12 Mins

Ingredients:

- 1 C. marinara sauce, divided
- 1 tbsp. capers, drained and divided
- 8 eggs
- ¼ C. whipping cream, divided
- ¼ C. Parmesan cheese, shredded and divided
- Salt and ground black pepper, as required

Directions:

1. Grease 4 ramekins. Set aside.
2. Divide the marinara sauce in the bottom of each prepared ramekin evenly and top with capers.
3. Carefully, crack 2 eggs over marinara sauce into each ramekin and top with cream, followed by the Parmesan cheese.
4. Sprinkle each ramekin with salt and black pepper.
5. Press "Power Button" of Ninja Foodi Digital Air Fry Oven and turn the dial to select the "Air Bake" mode.
6. Press the Time button and again turn the dial to set the cooking time to 12 minutes.
7. Now push the Temp button and rotate the dial to set the temperature at 400 degrees F.
8. Press "Start/Pause" button to start.
9. When the unit beeps to show that it is preheated, open the lid.
10. Arrange the ramekins over the "Wire Rack" and insert in the oven.
11. Serve warm.

Sweet Potato Tots

Servings: 4
Cooking Time: 1 Hour

Ingredients:

- 1 tbsp. of potato starch
- 2 small sweet potatoes, peeled
- 1-1/4 tsp. kosher salt
- 1/8 tsp. of garlic powder
- ¾ C. ketchup

Directions:

1. Boil water in a medium-sized pot over high heat.
2. Add the potatoes. Cook till it becomes tender. Transfer them to a plate for cooling. Grate them in a mid-sized bowl.
3. Toss gently with garlic powder, 1 tsp. of salt, and potato starch.
4. Shape the mix into tot-shaped cylinders.
5. Apply cooking spray on the air fryer basket.
6. Place half of the tots in a later in your basket. Apply some cooking spray.
7. Cook till it becomes light brown at 400°F.
8. Take out from the frying basket. Sprinkle some salt.
9. Serve with ketchup immediately.

Breakfast Frittata

Servings: 2
Cooking Time: 20 Mins

Ingredients:

- 4 eggs, beaten lightly
- 4 oz. sausages, cooked and crumbled
- 1 onion, chopped
- 2 tbsp. of red bell pepper, diced
- ½ C. shredded Cheddar cheese

Directions:

1. Bring together the cheese, eggs, sausage, onion, and bell pepper in a bowl.
2. Mix well.
3. Preheat your air fryer to 180 degrees C or 360 degrees F.
4. Apply cooking spray lightly.
5. Keep your egg mix in a prepared cake pan.
6. Now cook in your air fryer till the frittata has become set.

Tex-mex Hash Browns

Servings: 4

Cooking Time: 30 Mins

Ingredients:

- 1-1/2 24 oz. potatoes, cut and peeled
- 1 onion, cut into small pieces
- 1 tbsp. of olive oil
- 1 jalapeno, seeded and cut
- 1 red bell pepper, seeded and cut

Directions:

1. Soak the potatoes in water.
2. Preheat your air fryer to 160 degrees C or 320 degrees F.
3. Drain and dry the potatoes using a clean towel.
4. Keep in a bowl.
5. Drizzle some olive oil over the potatoes, coat well.
6. Transfer to the air frying basket.
7. Add the onion, jalapeno, and bell pepper in the bowl.
8. Sprinkle half tsp. olive oil, pepper, and salt. Coat well by tossing.
9. Now transfer your potatoes to the bowl with the veg mix from your fryer.
10. Place the empty basket into the air fryer. Raise the temperature to 180 degrees C or 356 degrees F.
11. Toss the contents of your bowl for mixing the potatoes with the vegetables evenly.
12. Transfer mix into the basket.
13. Cook until the potatoes have become crispy and brown.

Loaded Potatoes

Servings: 2
Cooking Time: 15 Mins

Ingredients:

- 11 oz. baby potatoes
- 2 cut bacon slices
- 1-1/2 oz. low-fat cheddar cheese, shredded
- 1 tsp. of olive oil
- 2 tbsp. low-fat sour cream

Directions:

1. Toss the potatoes with oil.
2. Place them in your air fryer basket. Cook till they get tender at 350°F. stir occasionally.
3. Cook the bacon meanwhile in a skillet till it gets crispy.
4. Take out the bacon from your pan. Crumble.
5. Keep the potatoes on a serving plate. Crush them lightly to split.
6. Top with cheese, chives, salt, crumbled bacon, and sour cream.

Potato Rosti

Servings: 2
Cooking Time: 15 Mins

Ingredients:

- ½ lb. potatoes, peeled, grated and squeezed
- ½ tbsp. fresh rosemary, chopped finely
- ½ tbsp. fresh thyme, chopped finely
- 1/8 tsp. red pepper flakes, crushed
- Salt and ground black pepper, as required
- 2 tbsp. butter, softened

Directions:

1. In a bowl, mix together the potato, herbs, red pepper flakes, salt and black pepper.
2. Press "Power Button" of Ninja Foodi Digital Air Fry Oven and turn the dial to select the "Air Fry" mode.
3. Press the Time button and again turn the dial to set the cooking time to 15 minutes.
4. Now push the Temp button and rotate the dial to set the temperature at 355 degrees F.
5. Press "Start/Pause" button to start.
6. When the unit beeps to show that it is preheated, open the lid and lightly, grease the sheet pan.
7. Arrange the potato mixture into the "Sheet Pan" and shape it into an even circle.
8. Insert the "Sheet Pan" in the oven.
9. Cut the potato rosti into wedges.
10. Top with the butter and serve immediately.

Spinach & Tomato Frittata

Servings: 6
Cooking Time: 30 Mins

Ingredients:

- 10 large eggs
- Salt and freshly ground black pepper, to taste
- 1 (5-oz.) bag baby spinach
- 2 C. grape tomatoes, halved
- 4 scallions, sliced thinly
- 8 oz. feta cheese, crumbled
- 3 tbsp. hot olive oil

Directions:

1. In a bowl, place the eggs, salt and black pepper and beat well.
2. Add the spinach, tomatoes, scallions and feta cheese and gently stir to combine.
3. Spread the oil in a baking pan and top with the spinach mixture.
4. Press "Power Button" of Ninja Foodi Digital Air Fry Oven and turn the dial to select "Air Bake" mode.
5. Press "Time Button" and again turn the dial to set the cooking time to 30 minutes.
6. Now push "Temp Button" and rotate the dial to set the temperature at 350 degrees F.
7. Press "Start/Pause" button to start.
8. When the unit beeps to show that it is preheated, open the lid.
9. Arrange pan over the wire rack and insert in the oven.
10. When cooking time is complete, open the lid and place the pan aside for about 5 minutes.
11. Cut into equal-sized wedges and serve hot.
12. Serving Suggestions: Enjoy your frittata with garlicky potatoes.
13. Variation Tip: Pick the right cheese for frittata.

Egg & Spinach Tart

Servings: 4
Cooking Time: 25 Mins

Ingredients:

- 1 puff pastry sheet, trimmed into a 9x13-inch rectangle
- 4 eggs
- ½ C. cheddar cheese, grated
- 7 cooked thick-cut bacon strips
- ½ C. cooked spinach
- 1 egg, lightly beaten

Directions:

1. Arrange the pastry in a lightly greased "Sheet Pan".
2. With a small knife gently, cut a 1-inch border around the edges of the puff pastry without cutting all the way through.
3. With a fork, pierce the center of pastry a few times.
4. Press "Power Button" of Ninja Foodi Digital Air Fry Oven and turn the dial to select the "Air Bake" mode.
5. Press the Time button and again turn the dial to set the cooking time to 10 minutes.
6. Now push the Temp button and rotate the dial to set the temperature at 400 degrees F.
7. Press "Start/Pause" button to start.
8. When the unit beeps to show that it is preheated, open the lid.
9. Insert the "Sheet Pan" in the oven.
10. Remove the "Sheet Pan" from oven and sprinkle the cheese over the center.
11. Place the spinach and bacon in an even layer across the tart.
12. Now, crack the eggs, leaving space between each one.
13. Press "Power Button" of Ninja Foodi Digital Air Fry Oven and turn the dial to select the "Air Bake" mode.
14. Press the Time button and again turn the dial to set the cooking time to 15 minutes.
15. Now push the Temp button and rotate the dial to set the temperature at 400 degrees F.
16. Press "Start/Pause" button to start.
17. When the unit beeps to show that it is preheated, open the lid.
18. Insert the "Sheet Pan" in the oven.
19. Remove the "Sheet Pan" from oven and set aside to cool for 2-3 minutes before cutting.
20. With a pizza cutter, cut into4 portions and serve.

Eggs In Bread Cups

Servings: 4
Cooking Time: 23 Mins

Ingredients:

- 4 bacon slices
- 2 bread slices, crust removed
- 4 eggs
- Salt and freshly ground black pepper, to taste

Directions:

1. Grease 4 C. of a muffin tin and set aside.
2. Heat a small frying pan over medium-high heat and cook the bacon slices for about 2-3 minutes.
3. With a slotted spoon, transfer the bacon slice onto a paper towel-lined plate to cool.
4. Break each bread slice in half.
5. Arrange 1 bread slices half in each of the prepared muffin C. and press slightly.
6. Now, arrange 1 bacon slice over each bread slice in a circular shape.
7. Crack 1 egg into each muffin C. and sprinkle with salt and black pepper.
8. Press "Power Button" of Ninja Foodi Digital Air Fry Oven and turn the dial to select "Air Bake" mode.
9. Press "Time Button" and again turn the dial to set the cooking time to 20 minutes.
10. Now push "Temp Button" and rotate the dial to set the temperature at 350 degrees F.
11. Press "Start/Pause" button to start.
12. When the unit beeps to show that it is preheated, open the lid.
13. Arrange the muffin tin over the wire rack and insert in the oven.
14. When cooking time is complete, open the lid and place the muffin tin onto a wire rack for about 10 minutes.
15. Serve warm.
16. Serving Suggestions: Feel free to top the bread C. with fresh herbs of your choice before serving.
17. Variation Tip: Pancetta can be used instead of bacon.

Garlic Cheese Bread

Servings: 2
Cooking Time: 10 Mins

Ingredients:

- 1 C. mozzarella cheese, shredded
- 1 large egg
- ¼ C. parmesan cheese, grated
- ½ tsp. garlic powder

Directions:

1. Use parchment paper to line your air fryer basket.
2. Bring together the parmesan cheese, mozzarella cheese, garlic powder, and egg in your bowl.
3. Mix until it combines well.
4. Now create a round circle on the parchment paper in your fryer basket.
5. Heat your air fryer to 175 degrees C or 350 degrees F.
6. Fry the bread. Take out and serve warm.

Cinnamon And Sugar Doughnuts

Servings: 9
Cooking Time: 16 Mins

Ingredients:

- 1 tsp. cinnamon
- 1/3 C. of white sugar
- 2 large egg yolks
- 2-1/2 tbsp. of butter, room temperature
- 1-1/2 tsp. baking powder
- 2-1/4 C. of all-purpose flour

Directions:

1. Take a bowl and press your butter and white sugar together in it.
2. Add the egg yolks. Stir till it combines well.
3. Now sift the baking powder, flour, and salt in another bowl.
4. Keep one-third of the flour mix and half of the sour cream into your egg-sugar mixture. Stir till it combines well.
5. Now mix the remaining sour cream and flour. Refrigerate till you can use it.
6. Bring together the cinnamon and one-third sugar in your bowl.
7. Roll half-inch-thick dough.
8. Cut large slices (9) in this dough. Create a small circle in the center. This will make doughnut shapes.
9. Preheat your fryer to 175 degrees C or 350 degrees F.
10. Brush melted butter on both sides of your doughnut.
11. Keep half of the doughnuts in the air fryer's basket.
12. Apply the remaining butter on the cooked doughnuts.
13. Dip into the sugar-cinnamon mix immediately.

Ham & Hash Brown Casserole

Servings: 5
Cooking Time: 35 Mins

Ingredients:

- 1½ tbsp. olive oil
- ½ of large onion, chopped
- 24 oz. frozen hash browns
- 3 eggs
- 2 tbsp. milk
- Salt and freshly ground black pepper, to taste
- ½ lb. ham, chopped
- ¼ C. Cheddar cheese, shredded

Directions:

1. In a skillet, heat the oil over medium heat and sauté the onion for about 4-5 minutes.
2. Remove from the heat and transfer the onion into a bowl.
3. Add the hash browns and mix well.
4. Place the mixture into a baking pan.
5. Press "Power Button" of Ninja Foodi Digital Air Fry Oven and turn the dial to select "Air Bake" mode.
6. Press "Time Button" and again turn the dial to set the cooking time to 32 minutes.
7. Now push "Temp Button" and rotate the dial to set the temperature at 350 degrees F.
8. Press "Start/Pause" button to start.
9. When the unit beeps to show that it is preheated, open the lid.
10. Arrange pan over the wire rack and insert in the oven.
11. Stir the mixture once after 8 minutes.
12. Meanwhile, in a bowl, add the eggs, milk, salt and black pepper and beat well.
13. After 15 minutes of cooking, place the egg mixture over hash brown mixture evenly and top with the ham.
14. After 30 minutes of cooking, sprinkle the casserole with the cheese.
15. When cooking time is complete, open the lid and place the casserole dish aside for about 5 minutes.
16. Cut into equal-sized wedges and serve.
17. Serving Suggestions: Avocado slices will accompany this casserole greatly.
18. Variation Tip: Use freshly shredded cheese.

Bell Pepper Omelet

Servings: 2
Cooking Time: 10 Mins

Ingredients:

- 1 tsp. butter
- 1 small onion, sliced
- ½ of green bell pepper, seeded and chopped
- 4 eggs
- ¼ tsp. milk
- Salt and ground black pepper, as required
- ¼ C. Cheddar cheese, grated

Directions:

1. In a skillet, melt the butter over medium heat and cook the onion and bell pepper for about 4-5 minutes.
2. Remove the skillet from heat and set aside to cool slightly.
3. Meanwhile, in a bowl, add the eggs, milk, salt and black pepper and beat well.
4. Add the cooked onion mixture and gently, stir to combine.
5. Place the zucchini mixture into a small baking pan.
6. Press "Power Button" of Ninja Foodi Digital Air Fry Oven and turn the dial to select the "Air Fry" mode.
7. Press the Time button and again turn the dial to set the cooking time to 5 minutes.
8. Now push the Temp button and rotate the dial to set the temperature at 355 degrees F.
9. Press "Start/Pause" button to start.
10. When the unit beeps to show that it is preheated, open the lid.
11. Arrange pan over the "Wire Rack" and insert in the oven.
12. Cut the omelet into 2 portions and serve hot.

Tomato Quiche

Servings: 2
Cooking Time: 30 Mins

Ingredients:

- 4 eggs
- ¼ C. onion, chopped
- ½ C. tomatoes, chopped
- ½ C. milk
- 1 C. Gouda cheese, shredded
- Salt, to taste

Directions:

1. In a small baking pan, add all the ingredients and mix well.
2. Press "Power Button" of Ninja Foodi Digital Air Fry Oven and turn the dial to select "Air Fry" mode.
3. Press "Time Button" and again turn the dial to set the cooking time to 30 minutes.
4. Now push "Temp Button" and rotate the dial to set the temperature at 340 degrees F.
5. Press "Start/Pause" button to start.
6. When the unit beeps to show that it is preheated, open the lid.
7. Arrange the pan over the wire rack and insert in the oven.
8. When cooking time is complete, open the lid and place the pan aside for about 5 minutes.
9. Cut into equal-sized wedges and serve.
10. Serving Suggestions: Fresh baby spring mix will be a great companion for this quiche.
11. Variation Tip: You can use any kind of fresh veggies for the filling of quiche.

Bacon & Spinach Muffins

Servings: 6
Cooking Time: 17 Mins

Ingredients:

- 6 eggs
- ½ C. milk
- Salt and freshly ground black pepper, to taste
- 1 C. fresh spinach, chopped
- 4 cooked bacon slices, crumbled

Directions:

1. In a bowl, add the eggs, milk, salt and black pepper and beat until well combined.
2. Add the spinach and stir to combine.
3. Divide the spinach mixture into 6 greased C. of an egg bite mold evenly.
4. Press "Power Button" of Ninja Foodi Digital Air Fry Oven and turn the dial to select "Air Fry" mode.
5. Press "Time Button" and again turn the dial to set the cooking time to 17 minutes.
6. Now push "Temp Button" and rotate the dial to set the temperature at 325 degrees F.
7. Press "Start/Pause" button to start.
8. When the unit beeps to show that it is preheated, open the lid.
9. Arrange the mold over the wire rack and insert in the oven.
10. When cooking time is complete, open the lid and place the mold onto a wire rack to cool for about 5 minutes.
11. Top with bacon pieces and serve warm.
12. Serving Suggestions: Serve these muffins with the drizzling of melted butter.
13. Variation Tip: Don't forget to grease the egg bite molds before pacing the egg mixture in them.

Cinnamon French Toasts

Servings: 2
Cooking Time: 5 Mins

Ingredients:

- 2 eggs
- ¼ C. whole milk
- 3 tbsp. sugar
- 2 tsp. olive oil
- 1/8 tsp. vanilla extract
- 1/8 tsp. ground cinnamon
- 4 bread slices

Directions:

1. In a large bowl, add all the ingredients except for bread slices and mix well.
2. Coat the bread slices with egg mixture evenly.
3. Press "Power Button" of Ninja Foodi Digital Air Fry Oven and turn the dial to select "Air Fry" mode.
4. Press "Time Button" and again turn the dial to set the cooking time to 6 minutes.
5. Now push "Temp Button" and rotate the dial to set the temperature at 390 degrees F.
6. Press "Start/Pause" button to start.
7. When the unit beeps to show that it is preheated, open the lid and lightly grease the sheet pan.
8. Arrange the bread slices into the air fry basket and insert in the oven.
9. Flip the bread slices once halfway through.
10. When cooking time is complete, open the lid and transfer the French toast onto serving plates.
11. Serve warm.
12. Serving Suggestions: You can enjoy these rench toast with the drizzling of maple syrup.
13. Variation Tip: For best result, soak the bread slices in egg mixture until each slice is thoroughly saturated.

Eggs In Avocado Cups

Servings: 2
Cooking Time: 10 Mins

Ingredients:

- 1 avocado, halved and pitted
- 2 large eggs
- Salt and freshly ground black pepper, to taste
- 2 cooked bacon slices, crumbled

Directions:

1. Carefully scoop out about 2 tsp. of flesh from each avocado half.
2. Crack 1 egg in each avocado half and sprinkle with salt and black pepper lightly.
3. Arrange avocado halves onto the greased piece of foil-lined sheet pan.
4. Press "Power Button" of Ninja Foodi Digital Air Fry Oven and turn the dial to select "Air Roast" mode.
5. Press "Time Button" and again turn the dial to set the cooking time to 10 minutes.
6. Now push "Temp Button" and rotate the dial to set the temperature at 375 degrees F.
7. Press "Start/Pause" button to start.
8. When the unit beeps to show that it is preheated, open the lid and insert the sheet pan in the oven.
9. When cooking time is complete, open the lid and transfer the avocado halves onto serving plates.
10. Top each avocado half with bacon pieces and serve.
11. Serving Suggestions: Serve these avocado halves with cherry tomatoes and fresh spinach.
12. Variation Tip: Smoked salmon can be replaced with bacon too.

French Toast Sticks

Servings: 2
Cooking Time: 10 Mins

Ingredients:

- 4 slices of thick bread
- 2 eggs, lightly beaten
- 1 tsp. cinnamon
- 1 tsp. of vanilla extract
- ¼ C. milk

Directions:

1. Cut the bread into slices for making sticks.
2. Keep parchment paper on the air fryer basket's bottom.
3. Preheat your air fryer to 180 degrees C or 360 degrees F.
4. Now stir together the milk, eggs, cinnamon, vanilla extract, and nutmeg (optional). Combine well.
5. Dip each bread piece into the egg mix. Submerge well.
6. Remove the excess fluid by shaking it well.
7. Keep them in the fryer basket in a single layer.
8. Cook without overcrowding your fryer.

Sausage Patties

Servings: 4
Cooking Time: 10 Mins

Ingredients:

- 1 pack sausage patties
- 1 serving cooking spray

Directions:

1. Preheat your air fryer to 200 degrees C or 400 degrees F.
2. Keep the sausage patties in a basket. Work in batches if needed.
3. Cook for 3 minutes.
4. Turn the sausage over and cook for another 2 minutes.

Roasted Cauliflower

Servings: 2

Cooking Time: 15 Mins

Ingredients:

- 4 C. of cauliflower florets
- 1 tbsp. peanut oil
- 3 cloves garlic
- ½ tsp. smoked paprika
- ½ tsp. of salt

Directions:

1. Preheat your air fryer to 200 degrees C or 400 degrees F.
2. Now cut the garlic into half. Use a knife to smash it.
3. Keep in a bowl with salt, paprika, and oil.
4. Add the cauliflower. Coat well.
5. Transfer the coated cauliflower to your air fryer.
6. Cook for 10 minutes. Shake after 5 minutes.

Snack & Dessert Recipes

Citrus Mousse

Servings: 2
Cooking Time: 12 Mins

Ingredients:
- For Mousse:
- 4 oz. cream cheese, softened
- ½ C. heavy cream
- 2 tbsp. fresh lime juice
- 2 tbsp. maple syrup
- Pinch of salt
- For Topping:
- 2 tbsp. heavy whipping cream

Directions:
1. For mousse: in a bowl, add all the ingredients and mix until well combined.
2. Transfer the mixture into 2 ramekins.
3. Press "Power Button" of Ninja Foodi Digital Air Fry Oven and turn the dial to select "Air Bake" mode.
4. Press "Time Button" and again turn the dial to set the cooking time to 12 minutes.
5. Now push "Temp Button" and rotate the dial to set the temperature at 350 degrees F.
6. Press "Start/Pause" button to start.
7. When the unit beeps to show that it is preheated, open the lid.
8. Arrange the ramekins over the wire rack and insert in the oven. When cooking time is complete, open the lid and place the ramekins aside to cool.
9. Refrigerate the ramekins for at least 3 hours before serving.
10. Top with heavy whipping cream and serve.
11. Serving Suggestions: serve with a garnishing of banana slices.
12. Variation Tip: Make sure to use freshly squeezed juice.

Nutty Pears

Servings: 2
Cooking Time: 30 Mins

Ingredients:

- 1 ripe Anjou pear, halved and cored
- 1/8 tsp. ground cinnamon
- 6 semisweet chocolate chips
- 2 tbsp. pecans, chopped
- 1 tsp. pure maple syrup

Directions:

1. Arrange the pear halves onto the greased sheet pan cut sides up and sprinkle with cinnamon.
2. Top each half with chocolate chips and pecans and drizzle with maple syrup.
3. Arrange a rack in the bottom position of Ninja Foodi Digital Air Fry Oven.
4. Press "Power Button" of Ninja Foodi Digital Air Fry Oven and turn the dial to select "Air Fry" mode.
5. Press "Time Button" and again turn the dial to set the cooking time to 30 minutes.
6. Now push "Temp Button" and rotate the dial to set the temperature at 350 degrees F.
7. Press "Start/Pause" button to start.
8. When the unit beeps to show that it is preheated, open the lid and insert the sheet pan in the oven.
9. When cooking time is complete, open the lid and transfer the pears onto a platter.
10. Serve warm.
11. Serving Suggestions: Sweet whipped cream will go great with these pears.
12. Variation Tip: Choose firm pears with the stem intact.

Banana Split

Servings: 8
Cooking Time: 14 Mins

Ingredients:

- 3 tbsp. coconut oil
- 1 C. panko breadcrumbs
- ½ C. corn flour
- 2 eggs
- 4 bananas, peeled and halved lengthwise
- 3 tbsp. sugar
- ¼ tsp. ground cinnamon
- 2 tbsp. walnuts, chopped

Directions:

1. In a medium skillet, melt the coconut oil over medium heat and cook breadcrumbs for about 3-4 minutes or until golden browned and crumbled, stirring continuously.
2. Transfer the breadcrumbs into a shallow bowl and set aside to cool.
3. In a second bowl, place the corn flour.
4. In a third bowl, whisk the eggs.
5. Coat the banana slices with flour and then, dip into eggs and finally, coat with the breadcrumbs evenly.
6. In a small bowl, mix together the sugar and cinnamon.
7. Press "Power Button" of Ninja Foodi Digital Air Fry Oven and turn the dial to select "Air Fry" mode.
8. Press "Time Button" and again turn the dial to set the cooking time to 10 minutes.
9. Now push "Temp Button" and rotate the dial to set the temperature at 280 degrees F.
10. Press "Start/Pause" button to start.
11. When the unit beeps to show that it is preheated, open the lid.
12. Arrange the banana slices into the air fry basket and sprinkle with cinnamon sugar.
13. Insert the basket in the oven.
14. When cooking time is complete, open the lid and transfer the banana slices onto plates to cool slightly
15. Sprinkle with chopped walnuts and serve.
16. Serving Suggestions: Serve with a scoop of strawberry ice cream.
17. Variation Tip: Pecans will be an excellent substitute for walnuts.

Chili Dip

Servings: 8
Cooking Time: 15 Mins

Ingredients:

- 1 (8-oz.) package cream cheese, softened
- 1 (16-oz.) can Hormel chili without beans
- 1 (16-oz.) package mild cheddar cheese, shredded

Directions:

1. In a baking pan, place the cream cheese and spread in an even layer.
2. Top with chili evenly, followed by the cheese.
3. Press "Power Button" of Ninja Foodi Digital Air Fry Oven and turn the dial to select "Air Bake" mode.
4. Press "Time Button" and again turn the dial to set the cooking time to 15 minutes.
5. Now push "Temp Button" and rotate the dial to set the temperature at 375 degrees F.
6. Press "Start/Pause" button to start.
7. When the unit beeps to show that it is preheated, open the lid.
8. Arrange pan over the wire rack and insert in the oven.
9. When cooking time is complete, open the lid.
10. Serve hot.
11. Serving Suggestions: serve this dip with tortilla chips or fresh veggies.
12. Variation Tip: Coby cheese can be replaced with cheddar cheese.

Easy Apple Pies

Servings: 10
Cooking Time: 15 Mins

Ingredients:

- 2 pie crusts
- 1 can apple pie filling
- 2 tbsp. of cinnamon sugar
- 1 egg, beaten

Directions:

1. Keep 1 pie crust on a floured surface.
2. Roll the dough out with your rolling pin.
3. Take a cookie-cutter. Now create 10 circles by cutting your pie crust.
4. Do this with the 2nd pie crust as well. You should have 20 circles.
5. Fill up half of each circle with the apple pie filling.
6. Keep the second circle on top, creating a mini pie. Make sure not to overfill.
7. Press down edges of your mini peas. Seal.
8. Brush beaten egg on the tops. Sprinkle some cinnamon sugar.
9. Preheat your air fryer to 175 degrees C or 360 degrees F.
10. Apply cooking spray on the fryer basket lightly.
11. Keep your mini peas in the basket. There should be space for air circulation.
12. Bake for 7 minutes. They should turn golden brown.

Glazed Figs

Servings: 4
Cooking Time: 10 Mins

Ingredients:
- 4 fresh figs
- 4 tsp. honey
- 2/3 C. Mascarpone cheese, softened
- Pinch of ground cinnamon

Directions:
1. Cut each fig into the quarter, leaving just a little at the base to hold the fruit together.
2. Arrange the figs onto a parchment paper-lined sheet pan and drizzle with honey.
3. Place about 2 tsp. of Mascarpone cheese in the center of each fig and sprinkle with cinnamon.
4. Press "Power Button" of Ninja Foodi Digital Air Fry Oven and turn the dial to select the "Air Broil" mode.
5. Press "Time Button" and again turn the dial to set the cooking time to 10 minutes.
6. Press "Start/Pause" button to start.
7. When the unit beeps to show that it is preheated, open the lid and insert the sheet pan in oven.
8. When cooking time is complete, open the lid and transfer the figs onto a platter.
9. Serve warm.
10. Serving Suggestions: Topping of chopped nuts will add a nice nutty texture.
11. Variation Tip: Select figs that are clean and dry, with smooth, unbroken skin.

Chicken Wings

Servings: 4
Cooking Time: 25 Mins

Ingredients:

- 1½ lb. chicken wingettes and drumettes
- 1/3 C. tomato sauce
- 2 tbsp. balsamic vinegar
- 2 tbsp. maple syrup
- ½ tsp. liquid smoke
- ¼ tsp. red pepper flakes, crushed
- Salt, as required

Directions:

1. Arrange the wings onto the greased "Sheet Pan".
2. Place the tofu mixture in the greased "Sheet Pan".
3. Press "Power Button" of Ninja Foodi Digital Air Fry Oven and turn the dial to select the "Air Fry" mode.
4. Press the Time button and again turn the dial to set the cooking time to 25 minutes.
5. Now push the Temp button and rotate the dial to set the temperature at 380 degrees F.
6. Press "Start/Pause" button to start.
7. When the unit beeps to show that it is preheated, open the lid.
8. Insert the "Sheet Pan" in oven.
9. Meanwhile, in a small pan, add the remaining ingredients over medium heat and cook for about 10 minutes, stirring occasionally.
10. Remove from oven and place the chicken wings into a bowl.
11. Add the sauce and toss to coat well.
12. Serve immediately.

Spicy Spinach Chips

Servings: 4
Cooking Time: 10 Mins

Ingredients:

- 2 C. fresh spinach leaves, torn into bite-sized pieces
- ½ tbsp. coconut oil, melted
- 1/8 tsp. garlic powder
- Salt, as required

Directions:

1. In a large bowl and mix together all the ingredients.
2. Arrange the spinach pieces onto the greased "Sheet Pan".
3. Press "Power Button" of Ninja Foodi Digital Air Fry Oven and turn the dial to select the "Air Fry" mode.
4. Press the Time button and again turn the dial to set the cooking time to 10 minutes.
5. Now push the Temp button and rotate the dial to set the temperature at 300 degrees F.
6. Press "Start/Pause" button to start.
7. When the unit beeps to show that it is preheated, open the lid.
8. Insert the "Sheet Pan" in oven.
9. Toss the spinach chips once halfway through.

Air Fryer Beignets

Servings: 7
Cooking Time: 15 Mins

Ingredients:

- ½ C. all-purpose flour
- 1 egg, separated
- ½ tsp. of baking powder
- 1-1/2 tsp. melted butter
- ¼ C. white sugar
- ½ tsp. of vanilla extract

Directions:

1. Preheat your air fryer to 185 degrees C or 370 degrees F.
2. Whisk together the sugar, flour, butter, egg yolk, vanilla extract, baking powder, salt, and water in a bowl. Combine well by stirring.
3. Use an electric hand mixer to beat the white portion of the egg in a bowl.
4. Fold this into the batter.
5. Now use a small ice cream scoop to add the mold.
6. Keep the mold into the air fryer basket.
7. Fry for 10 minutes in your air fryer.
8. Take out the mold and the pop beignets carefully.
9. Flip them over on a round of parchment paper.
10. Now transfer the parchment round with the beignets into the fryer basket.
11. Cook for 4 more minutes.

Air Fryer Oreos

Servings: 9
Cooking Time: 10 Mins

Ingredients:
- ½ C. pancake mix
- 9 chocolate sandwich cookies like Oreo®
- 1/3 C. water
- 1 tbsp. of confectioners' sugar

Directions:
1. Mix water and the pancake mix. Combine well.
2. Use parchment paper to line the basket of your air fryer.
3. Apply some cooking spray.
4. Now dip the cookies into your pancake mix. Keep in the fryer basket.
5. They should not touch each other.
6. Preheat your air fryer to 200 degrees C or 400 degrees F.
7. Cook for 4 minutes.
8. Flip over. Cook for 3 more minutes until they turn golden brown.
9. Sprinkle some confectioners' sugar.

Basic Hot Dogs

Servings: 4
Cooking Time: 5 Mins

Ingredients:
- 4 hot dogs
- 4 hot dog buns

Directions:
1. Preheat your air fryer to 200 degrees C or 390 degrees F.
2. Keep the buns in your fryer basket. Cook for 2-3 minutes.
3. Transfer them to a plate.
4. Keep your hot dogs in the air fryer basket. Cook for 3 minutes.
5. Place them in the buns.

Banana Cake

Servings: 4
Cooking Time: 30 Mins

Ingredients:

- 1 mashed banana
- 1 egg
- 1/3 C. brown sugar
- 3-1/2 tbsp. of butter, room temperature
- 1 C. flour
- 2 tbsp. of honey

Directions:

1. Preheat your air fryer to 160 degrees C or 320 degrees F.
2. Apply cooking spray on a small tube pan.
3. Beat the butter and sugar together in your bowl. It should turn creamy.
4. Bring together the egg, banana, and honey in another bowl.
5. Now whisk this banana mix into your butter mixture. It should be smooth.
6. Stir in the salt and flour into this mixture.
7. Mix the batter until it gets smooth.
8. Keep in the pan and transfer to the air fryer basket.
9. Bake until you see a toothpick coming out clean from the cake.

Garlic-parsley Baby Potatoes

Servings: 4
Cooking Time: 20 Mins

Ingredients:

- 1 oz. baby potatoes, cut into small quarters
- ½ tsp. garlic, granulated
- 1 tbsp. of avocado oil
- ½ tsp. parsley, dried
- ¼ tsp. salt

Directions:

1. Preheat your air fryer to 175 degrees C or 350 degrees F.
2. Combine the oil and potatoes in your bowl. Coat well by tossing.
3. Include ¼ tsp. of parsley and ¼ tsp. of granulated garlic.
4. Repeat the same process for the remaining parsley and garlic.
5. Transfer potatoes to the basket of your air fryer.
6. Cook for 20 minutes, tossing occasionally. It should turn golden brown.

Cheese Pastries

Servings: 6
Cooking Time: 10 Mins

Ingredients:

- 1 egg yolk
- 4 oz. feta cheese, crumbled
- 1 scallion, finely chopped
- 2 tbsp. fresh parsley, finely chopped
- Salt and freshly ground black pepper, to taste
- 2 frozen phyllo pastry sheets, thawed
- 2 tbsp. olive oil

Directions:

1. In a large bowl, add the egg yolk, and beat well.
2. Add the feta cheese, scallion, parsley, salt, and black pepper and mix well.
3. Cut each pastry sheet in three strips.
4. Add about 1 tsp. of feta mixture on the underside of a strip.
5. Fold the tip of the pastry sheet over the filling in a zigzag manner to form a triangle.
6. Repeat with the remaining strips and fillings.
7. Coat each pastry with oil evenly.
8. Press "Power Button" of Ninja Foodi Digital Air Fry Oven and turn the dial to select "Air Fry" mode.
9. Press "Time Button" and again turn the dial to set the cooking time to 3 minutes.
10. Now push "Temp Button" and rotate the dial to set the temperature at 390 degrees F.
11. Press "Start/Pause" button to start.
12. When the unit beeps to show that it is preheated, open the lid.
13. Arrange the pastries in the air fry basket and insert in the oven.
14. After 3 minutes, set the temperature at 390 degrees F for 2 minutes.
15. When cooking time is complete, open the lid and transfer the pastries onto a platter.
16. Serve warm.
17. Serving Suggestions: Serve these pastries with marinara sauce.
18. Variation Tip: Feta cheese can be replaced with ricotta cheese too.

Plum Crisp

Servings: 2
Cooking Time: 40 Mins

Ingredients:

- 1½ C. plums, pitted and sliced
- ¼ C. sugar, divided
- 1½ tsp. cornstarch
- 3 tbsp. flour
- ¼ tsp. ground cinnamon
- Pinch of salt
- 1½ tbsp. cold butter, chopped
- 3 tbsp. rolled oats

Directions:

1. In a bowl, place plum slices, 1 tsp. of sugar and cornstarch and toss to coat well.
2. Divide the plum mixture into lightly greased 2 (8-oz.) ramekins.
3. In a bowl, mix together the flour, remaining sugar, cinnamon and salt.
4. With a pastry blender, cut in bitterer until a crumbly mixture forms.
5. Add the oats and gently stir to combine.
6. Place the oat mixture over plum slices into each ramekin.
7. Press "Power Button" of Ninja Foodi Digital Air Fry Oven and turn the dial to select "Air Bake" mode.
8. Press "Time Button" and again turn the dial to set the cooking time to 40 minutes.
9. Now push "Temp Button" and rotate the dial to set the temperature at 350 degrees F.
10. Press "Start/Pause" button to start.
11. When the unit beeps to show that it is preheated, open the lid.
12. Arrange the ramekins over the wire rack and insert in the oven.
13. When cooking time is complete, open the lid and place the ramekins onto a wire rack to cool for about 10 minutes.
14. Serve warm.
15. Serving Suggestions: Vanilla ice cream will go great with crisp.
16. Variation Tip: Select plums with a sweet aroma and free of bruises and faded spots.

Apple Pies

Servings: 4
Cooking Time: 15 Mins

Ingredients:

- 2 medium apples, diced
- 6 tbsp. brown sugar
- 1 tsp. of cornstarch
- 4 tbsp. butter
- ½ tbsp. of grapeseed oil
- 1 tsp. milk

Directions:

1. Combine butter, apples, and brown sugar in your non-stick skillet.
2. Cook on medium heat for 5 minutes. The apples should get soft.
3. Now dissolve the cornstarch in some cold water.
4. Stir the apple mixture in. Cook until you see the sauce thickening.
5. Take out the apple pie filling. Keep aside for cooling.
6. Unroll your pie crust on a floured surface. Roll out a bit to make the dough surface smooth.
7. Cut your dough into small rectangles. 2 of them should fit into the air fryer.
8. Repeat the process until there are 8 rectangles that are equal.
9. Use water to wet the outer edges of your 4 rectangles.
10. Keep the apple filling at the center. It should be half an inch away from the edges.
11. Roll out your other rectangles. They should be a bit bigger than the ones you have filled up.
12. Keep these rectangles at the top of your filling.
13. Use a fork to crimp the edges for sealing.
14. Now create four small slits at the top portion of your pies.
15. Apply some cooking spray in the air fryer basket.
16. Brush grapeseed oil on the top portion of 2 pies. Keep them in the fryer basket.
17. Bake for 6 minutes. They should become golden brown.
18. Take them out. Repeat with the other 2 pies.
19. Drizzle some milk on the warm pies. Let them dry before serving.

Cheddar Biscuits

Servings: 8
Cooking Time: 10 Mins

Ingredients:

- 1/3 C. unbleached all-purpose flour
- 1/8 tsp. cayenne pepper
- 1/8 tsp. smoked paprika
- Pinch of garlic powder
- Salt and freshly ground black pepper, to taste
- ½ C. sharp cheddar cheese, shredded
- 2 tbsp. butter, softened
- Nonstick cooking spray

Directions:

1. In a food processor, add the flour, spices, salt and black pepper and pulse until well combined.
2. Add the cheese and butter and pulse until a smooth dough forms.
3. Place the dough onto a lightly floured surface.
4. Make 16 small equal-sized balls from the dough and press each slightly.
5. Press "Power Button" of Ninja Foodi Digital Air Fry Oven and turn the dial to select "Air Bake" mode.
6. Press "Time Button" and again turn the dial to set the cooking time to 10 minutes.
7. Now push "Temp Button" and rotate the dial to set the temperature at 330 degrees F.
8. Press "Start/Pause" button to start.
9. When the unit beeps to show that it is preheated, open the lid and grease the air fry basket.
10. Arrange the biscuits into the prepared air fry basket and insert in the oven.
11. When cooking time is complete, open the lid and place the basket onto a wire rack for about 10 minutes.
12. Carefully invert the biscuits onto the wire rack to cool completely before serving.
13. Serving Suggestions: Serve these cheddar biscuits with the drizzling of garlic butter.
14. Variation Tip: For flaky layers, use cold butter.

Roasted Bananas

Servings: 1
Cooking Time: 7 Mins

Ingredients:
- 1 banana, sliced into diagonal pieces
- Avocado oil cooking spray

Directions:
1. Take parchment paper and line the air fryer basket with it.
2. Preheat your air fryer to 190 degrees C or 375 degrees F.
3. Keep your slices of banana in the basket. They should not touch.
4. Apply avocado oil to mist the slices of banana.
5. Cook for 5 minutes.
6. Take out the basket. Flip the slices carefully.
7. Cook for 2 more minutes. The slices of banana should be caramelized and browning. Take them out from the basket.

Spicy Chickpeas

Servings: 4
Cooking Time: 10 Mins

Ingredients:

- 1 (15-oz.) can chickpeas, rinsed and drained
- 1 tbsp. olive oil
- ½ tsp. cayenne pepper
- ½ tsp. smoked paprika
- ½ tsp. ground cumin
- 1/8 tsp. ground cinnamon
- Salt, to taste

Directions:

1. In a bowl, add all the ingredients and toss to coat well.
2. Press "Power Button" of Ninja Foodi Digital Air Fry Oven and turn the dial to select "Air Fry" mode.
3. Press "Time Button" and again turn the dial to set the cooking time to 10 minutes.
4. Now push "Temp Button" and rotate the dial to set the temperature at 390 degrees F.
5. Press "Start/Pause" button to start.
6. When the unit beeps to show that it is preheated, open the lid.
7. Arrange the chickpeas into the air fry basket and insert in the oven.
8. When cooking time is complete, open the lid and transfer the chickpeas into a bowl.
9. Serve warm.
10. Serving Suggestions: These roasted chickpeas can also be used as a topping of potato soup.
11. Variation Tip: You can adjust the ratio of spices according to your taste.

Beef Taquitos

Servings: 6
Cooking Time: 8 Mins

Ingredients:

- 6 corn tortillas
- 2 C. cooked beef, shredded
- ½ C. onion, chopped
- 1 C. pepper jack cheese, shredded
- Olive oil cooking spray

Directions:

1. Arrange the tortillas onto a smooth surface.
2. Place the shredded meat over one corner of each tortilla, followed by onion and cheese.
3. Roll each tortilla to secure the filling and secure with toothpicks.
4. Spray each taquito with cooking spray evenly.
5. Arrange the taquitos onto the greased "Sheet Pan".
6. Place the tofu mixture in the greased "Sheet Pan".
7. Press "Power Button" of Ninja Foodi Digital Air Fry Oven and turn the dial to select the "Air Fry" mode.
8. Press the Time button and again turn the dial to set the cooking time to 8 minutes.
9. Now push the Temp button and rotate the dial to set the temperature at 400 degrees F.
10. Press "Start/Pause" button to start.
11. When the unit beeps to show that it is preheated, open the lid.
12. Insert the "Sheet Pan" in oven.
13. Serve warm.

Meat Recipes

Spiced Flank Steak

Servings: 6
Cooking Time: 12 Mins

Ingredients:

- 2 tbsp. balsamic vinegar
- 2 tbsp. olive oil
- 3 garlic cloves, minced
- 1 tsp. red chili powder
- 1 tsp. ground cumin
- 1 tsp. onion powder
- Salt and freshly ground black pepper, to taste
- 1 (2-pound) flank steak

Directions:

1. In a large bowl, mix together the vinegar, spices, salt and black pepper.
2. Add the steak and coat with mixture generously.
3. Cover the bowl and place in the refrigerator for at least 1 hour.
4. Remove the steak from bowl and place onto the greased sheet pan.
5. Press "Power Button" of Ninja Foodi Digital Air Fry Oven and turn the dial to select the "Air Broil" mode.
6. Press "Time Button" and again turn the dial to set the cooking time to 12 minutes.
7. Press "Start/Pause" button to start.
8. When the unit beeps to show that it is preheated, open the lid and insert the sheet pan in the oven.
9. Flip the steak once halfway through.
10. When cooking time is complete, open the lid and place the steak onto a cutting board.
11. With a sharp knife, cut the steak into desired sized slices and serve.
12. Serving Suggestions: Enjoy this steak with a drizzling of fresh lemon juice.
13. Variation Tip: choose the steak that is as uniform in thickness.

Pork Skewers with Mango Salsa & Black Bean

Servings: 4

Cooking Time: 10 Mins

Ingredients:

- 1 lb. pork tenderloin, cut into small cubes
- ½ can black beans, rinsed and drained
- 1 mango, peeled, seeded, and chopped
- 4-1/2 tsp. of onion powder
- 4-1/2 tsp. thyme, crushed
- 1 tbsp. vegetable oil
- ¼ tsp. cloves, ground

Directions:

1. Stir in the thyme, onion powder, salt, and cloves in a bowl to create the seasoning mixture.
2. Keep a tbsp. of this for the pork. Transfer the remaining to an airtight container for later.
3. Preheat your air fryer to 175 degrees C or 350 degrees F.
4. Thread the chunks of pork into the skewers.
5. Brush oil on the pork. Sprinkle the seasoning mix on all sides.
6. Keep in your air fryer basket.
7. Cook for 5 minutes.
8. Mash one-third of the mango in your bowl in the meantime.
9. Stir the remaining mango in, and also salt, pepper, and black beans.
10. Serve the salsa with the pork skewers.

Glazed Lamb Meatballs

Servings: 8
Cooking Time: 30 Mins

Ingredients:
- For Meatballs:
- 2 lb. lean ground lamb
- 2/3 C. quick-cooking oats
- ½ C. Ritz crackers, crushed
- 1 (5-oz.) can evaporated milk
- 2 large eggs, beaten lightly
- 1 tsp. maple syrup
- 1 tbsp. dried onion, minced
- Salt and freshly ground black pepper, to taste
- For Sauce:
- 1/3 C. orange marmalade
- 1/3 C. maple syrup
- 1/3 C. sugar
- 2 tbsp. cornstarch
- 2 tbsp. soy sauce
- 1-2 tbsp. Sriracha
- 1 tbsp. Worcestershire sauce

Directions:
1. For meatballs: in a large bowl, add all the ingredients and mix until well combined.
2. Make 1½-inch balls from the mixture.
3. Arrange half of the meatballs onto the greased sheet pan in a single layer.
4. Press "Power Button" of Ninja Foodi Digital Air Fry Oven and turn the dial to select "Air Fry" mode.
5. Press "Time Button" and again turn the dial to set the cooking time to 15 minutes.
6. Now push "Temp Button" and rotate the dial to set the temperature at 380 degrees F.
7. Press "Start/Pause" button to start.
8. When the unit beeps to show that it is preheated, open the lid and insert the sheet pan in the oven.
9. Flip the meatballs once halfway through.
10. When cooking time is complete, open the lid and transfer the meatballs into a bowl.
11. Repeat with the remaining meatballs.
12. Meanwhile, for sauce: in a small pan, add all the ingredients over medium heat and cook until thickened, stirring continuously.
13. Serve the meatballs with the topping of sauce.
14. Serving Suggestions: Mashed buttery potatoes make a classic pairing with meatballs.
15. Variation Tip: You can adjust the ratio of sweetener according to your taste.

Roast Beef

Servings: 6
Cooking Time: 45 Mins

Ingredients:

- 2 oz. beef roast
- 1 tbsp. olive oil
- 2 tsp. thyme and rosemary
- 1 tsp. of salt
- 1 onion, medium

Directions:

1. Preheat your air fryer to 200 degrees C or 390 degrees F.
2. Mix the rosemary, oil, and salt on a plate.
3. Use paper towels to pat dry your beef roast.
4. Keep it on a plate. Coat the oil-herb mix on the outside.
5. Keep your beef roast in the air fryer basket.
6. Peel the onion. Cut it in half. Keep the halves next to your roast.
7. Cook for 12 minutes.
8. Change the temperature to 180 degrees C or 360 degrees F.
9. Cook for another 25 minutes.
10. Take it out and cover using kitchen foil.
11. Let it rest for 5 minutes.
12. Carve it thinly against the grain.
13. Serve with steamed or roasted vegetables, gravy, and wholegrain mustard.

Buttered Rib-eye Steak

Servings: 3
Cooking Time: 14 Mins

Ingredients:

- 2 (8-oz.) rib-eye steaks
- 2 tbsp. butter, melted
- Salt and freshly ground black pepper, to taste

Directions:

1. Coat the steak with butter and then sprinkle with salt and black pepper evenly.
2. Press "Power Button" of Ninja Foodi Digital Air Fry Oven and turn the dial to select "Air Roast" mode.
3. Press "Time Button" and again turn the dial to set the cooking time to 14 minutes.
4. Now push "Temp Button" and rotate the dial to set the temperature at 400 degrees F.
5. Press "Start/Pause" button to start.
6. When the unit beeps to show that it is preheated, open the lid and grease the air fry basket.
7. Arrange the steaks into the air fry basket and insert in the oven.
8. When cooking time is complete, open the lid and place steaks onto a platter for about 5 minutes.
9. Cut each steak into desired sized slices and serve.
10. Serving Suggestions: Enjoy this steak with grille potatoes.
11. Variation Tip: Rib-eye steak is best when it's cooked medium-rare.

Bbq Baby Ribs

Servings: 4
Cooking Time: 35 Mins

Ingredients:

- 3 lb. ribs of baby back pork
- 1 tbsp. each of white and brown sugar
- 1 tsp. smoked paprika
- 1 tsp. of garlic, granulated
- 1/3 C. barbeque sauce

Directions:

1. Preheat your air fryer to 175 degrees C or 350 degrees F.
2. Strip off the membrane from the rib's back. Cut into 4 equal size portions.
3. Bring together the brown and white sugar, paprika, pepper, granulated garlic, and the green seasoning (optional) in a bowl.
4. Rub the spice mix all over your pork ribs.
5. Keep in the fryer basket.
6. Now cook the ribs for 25 minutes. Turn once after 12 minutes.
7. Brush the BBQ sauce.
8. Air fry this for another 5 minutes.

Italian-style Meatballs

Servings: 12
Cooking Time: 35 Mins

Ingredients:

- 10 oz. lean beef, ground
- 3 garlic cloves, minced
- 5 oz. turkey sausage
- 2 tbsp. shallot, minced
- 1 large egg, lightly beaten
- 2 tbsp. of olive oil
- 1 tbsp. of rosemary and thyme, chopped

Directions:

1. Preheat your air fryer to 400 degrees F.
2. Heat oil and add the shallot. Cook for 1-2 minutes.
3. Add the garlic now and cook. Take out from the heat.
4. Add the garlic and cooked shallot along with the egg, turkey sausage, beef, rosemary, thyme, and salt. Combine well by stirring.
5. Shape the mixture gently into 1-1/2 inch small balls.
6. Keep the balls in your air fryer basket.
7. Cook your meatballs at 400 degrees F. They should turn light brown.
8. Take out. Keep warm.
9. Serve the meatballs over rice or pasta.

Simple Beef Tenderloin

Servings: 10
Cooking Time: 50 Mins

Ingredients:

- 1 (3½-pound) beef tenderloin, trimmed
- 2 tbsp. olive oil
- Salt and ground black pepper, as required

Directions:

1. With kitchen twine, tie the tenderloin.
2. Rub the tenderloin with oil and season with salt and black pepper.
3. Place the tenderloin into the greased baking pan.
4. Press "Power Button" of Ninja Foodi Digital Air Fry Oven and turn the dial to select the "Air Roast" mode.
5. Press the Time button and again turn the dial to set the cooking time to 50 minutes.
6. Now push the Temp button and rotate the dial to set the temperature at 400 degrees F.
7. Press "Start/Pause" button to start.
8. When the unit beeps to show that it is preheated, open the lid and insert baking pan in the oven.
9. Remove from oven and place the tenderloin onto a platter for about 10 minutes before slicing.
10. With a sharp knife, cut the tenderloin into desired sized slices and serve.

Mushrooms With Steak

Servings: 4

Cooking Time: 10 Mins

Ingredients:

- 1 oz. sirloin beef steak, cut into small 1-inch cubes
- ¼ C. Worcestershire sauce
- 8 oz. sliced button mushrooms
- 1 tbsp. of olive oil
- 1 tsp. chili flakes, crushed

Directions:

1. Combine the mushrooms, steak, olive oil Worcestershire sauce, and chili flakes in your bowl.
2. Keep it refrigerated for 4 hours minimum.
3. Take out 30 minutes before cooking.
4. Preheat your oven to 200 degrees C or 400 degrees F.
5. Drain out the marinade from your steak mixture.
6. Now keep the mushrooms and steak in the air fryer basket.
7. Cook for 5 minutes in the air fryer.
8. Toss and then cook for another 5 minutes.
9. Transfer the mushrooms and steak to a serving plate.

Braised Lamb Shanks

Servings: 4
Cooking Time: 2 Hours, 30 Mins

Ingredients:

- 4 lamb shanks
- 4 crushed garlic cloves
- 2 tbsp. of olive oil
- 3 C. of beef broth
- 2 tbsp. balsamic vinegar

Directions:

1. Rub pepper and salt on your lamb shanks. Keep in the baking pan.
2. Rub the smashed garlic on the lamb well.
3. Now cut the shanks with olive oil.
4. Keep underneath your lamb.
5. Keep the pan into the rack.
6. Roast for 20 minutes at 425 degrees F. Change to low for 2 hours at 250 F.
7. Add vinegar and 2 C. of broth.
8. Including the remaining broth after the 1st hour.

Herbed Pork Chops

Servings: 3
Cooking Time: 12 Mins

Ingredients:

- 2 garlic cloves, minced
- ½ tbsp. fresh cilantro, chopped
- ½ tbsp. fresh rosemary, chopped
- ½ tbsp. fresh parsley, chopped
- 2 tbsp. olive oil
- ¾ tbsp. Dijon mustard
- 1 tbsp. ground coriander
- 1 tsp. sugar
- Salt, to taste
- 3 (6-oz.) (1-inch thick) pork chops

Directions:

1. In a bowl, mix together the garlic, herbs, oil, mustard, coriander, sugar, and salt.
2. Add the pork chops and coat with marinade generously.
3. Cover the bowl and refrigerate for about 2-3 hours.
4. Remove chops from the refrigerator and set aside at room temperature for about 30 minutes.
5. Press "Power Button" of Ninja Foodi Digital Air Fry Oven and turn the dial to select "Air Fry" mode.
6. Press "Time Button" and again turn the dial to set the cooking time to 12 minutes.
7. Now push "Temp Button" and rotate the dial to set the temperature at 390 degrees F.
8. Press "Start/Pause" button to start.
9. When the unit beeps to show that it is preheated, open the lid and grease the air fry basket.
10. Arrange chops into the prepared Air Fryer basket in a single layer and insert in the oven.
11. When cooking time is complete, open the lid and transfer the chops onto plates.
12. Serve hot.
13. Serving Suggestions: Serve thee chops with curried potato salad.
14. Variation Tip: Bring the pork chops to room temperature before cooking.

Sweet Potato, Brown Rice, And Lamb

Servings: 2

Cooking Time: 10 Mins

Ingredients:

- ¼ C. lamb, cooked and puréed
- ½ C. cooked brown rice
- ¼ C. of sweet potato purée

Directions:

1. Keep all the ingredients in your bowl.
2. Pulse until you achieve the desired consistency.
3. Process with milk to get a smoother consistency.
4. Store in an airtight container. Refrigerate.

Spiced Pork Shoulder

Servings: 6
Cooking Time: 55 Mins

Ingredients:

- 1 tsp. ground cumin
- 1 tsp. cayenne pepper
- ½ tsp. garlic powder
- ½ tsp. onion powder
- Salt and ground black pepper, as required
- 2 lb. skin-on pork shoulder

Directions:

1. In a small bowl, place the spices, salt and black pepper and mix well.
2. Arrange the pork shoulder onto a cutting board, skin-side down.
3. Season the inner side of pork shoulder with salt and black pepper.
4. With kitchen twines, tie the pork shoulder into a long round cylinder shape.
5. Season the outer side of pork shoulder with spice mixture.
6. Press "Power Button" of Ninja Foodi Digital Air Fry Oven and turn the dial to select the "Air Roast" mode.
7. Press the Time button and again turn the dial to set the cooking time to 55 minutes.
8. Now push the Temp button and rotate the dial to set the temperature at 350 degrees F.
9. Press "Start/Pause" button to start.
10. When the unit beeps to show that it is preheated, open the lid and grease "Air Fry Basket".
11. Arrange the pork shoulder into "Air Fry Basket" and insert in the oven.
12. Remove from oven and place the pork shoulder onto a platter for about 10 minutes before slicing.
13. With a sharp knife, cut the pork shoulder into desired sized slices and serve.

Seasoned Sirloin Steak

Servings: 2
Cooking Time: 12 Mins

Ingredients:

- 2 (7-oz.) top sirloin steak
- 1 tbsp. steak seasoning
- Salt and ground black pepper, as required

Directions:

1. Season each steak with steak seasoning, salt and black pepper.
2. Arrange the steaks onto the greased cooking pan.
3. Press "Power Button" of Ninja Foodi Digital Air Fry Oven and turn the dial to select the "Air Fry" mode.
4. Press the Time button and again turn the dial to set the cooking time to 12 minutes.
5. Now push the Temp button and rotate the dial to set the temperature at 400 degrees F.
6. Press "Start/Pause" button to start.
7. When the unit beeps to show that it is preheated, open the lid and insert baking pan in the oven.
8. Flip the steaks once halfway through.
9. Remove from oven and serve.

Lamb Sirloin Steak

Servings: 4
Cooking Time: 15 Mins

Ingredients:
- 1 oz. lamb sirloin steaks, boneless
- 5 garlic cloves
- 1 tsp. fennel, ground
- ½ onion
- 1 tsp. cinnamon, ground

Directions:
1. Add all the ingredients in your blender bowl other than the lamb chops.
2. Pulse and blend until you see the onion minced fine. All the ingredients should be blended well.
3. Now keep your lamb chops in a big-sized bowl.
4. Slash the meat and fat with a knife.
5. The marinade should penetrate.
6. Include the spice paste. Mix well.
7. Refrigerate the mixture for half an hour.
8. Keep the steaks of lamb in your air fryer basket.
9. Cook, flipping once.

Pork Meatloaf

Servings: 8
Cooking Time: 1 Hour 5 Mins

Ingredients:

- For Meatloaf:
- 2 lb. lean ground pork
- 1 C. quick-cooking oats
- ½ C. carrot, peeled and shredded
- 1 medium onion, chopped
- ½ C. fat-free milk
- ¼ of egg, beaten
- 2 tbsp. ketchup
- 1 tsp. garlic powder
- ¼ tsp. ground black pepper
- For Topping:
- ¼ C. ketchup
- ¼ C. quick-cooking oats

Directions:

1. For meatloaf: in a bowl, add all the ingredients and mix until well combined.
2. For topping: in another bowl, add all the ingredients and mix until well combined.
3. Transfer the mixture into a greased loaf pan and top with the topping mixture.
4. Press "Power Button" of Ninja Foodi Digital Air Fry Oven and turn the dial to select "Air Bake" mode.
5. Press "Time Button" and again turn the dial to set the cooking time to 65 minutes.
6. Now push "Temp Button" and rotate the dial to set the temperature at 350 degrees F.
7. Press "Start/Pause" button to start.
8. When the unit beeps to show that it is preheated, open the lid.
9. Arrange the loaf pan over the wire rack and insert in the oven.
10. When cooking time is complete, open the lid and place the loaf pan onto a wire rack for about 10 minutes.
11. Carefully invert the loaf onto the wire rack.
12. Cut into desired sized slices and serve.
13. Serving Suggestions: Baked cauliflower will nicely accompany this meatloaf.
14. Variation Tip: Add in a sprinkling of Italian seasoning in meatloaf.

Poultry Recipes

Roasted Cornish Game Hen

Servings: 4
Cooking Time: 16 Mins

Ingredients:

- ¼ C. olive oil
- 1 tsp. fresh rosemary, chopped
- 1 tsp. fresh thyme, chopped
- 1 tsp. fresh lemon zest, finely grated
- ¼ tsp. sugar
- ¼ tsp. red pepper flakes, crushed
- Salt and freshly ground black pepper, to taste
- 2 lb. Cornish game hen, backbone removed and halved

Directions:

1. In a bowl, mix together oil, herbs, lemon zest, sugar, and spices.
2. Add the hen portions and coat with the marinade generously.
3. Cover and refrigerate for about 24 hours.
4. In a strainer, place the hen portions and set aside to drain any liquid.
5. Press "Power Button" of Ninja Foodi Digital Air Fry Oven and turn the dial to select "Air Fry" mode.
6. Press "Time Button" and again turn the dial to set the cooking time to 16 minutes.
7. Now push "Temp Button" and rotate the dial to set the temperature at 390 degrees F.
8. Press "Start/Pause" button to start.
9. When the unit beeps to show that it is preheated, open the lid and grease the air fry basket.
10. Arrange the hen portions into the prepared basket and insert in the oven.
11. When cooking time is complete, open the lid and transfer the hen portions onto a platter.
12. Cut each portion in half and serve.
13. Serving Suggestions: Serve with dinner rolls.
14. Variation Tip: Place the hens in the basket, breast side up.

Garlicky Duck Legs

Servings: 2
Cooking Time: 30 Mins

Ingredients:

- 2 garlic cloves, minced
- 1 tbsp. fresh parsley, chopped
- 1 tsp. five-spice powder
- Salt and freshly ground black pepper, to taste
- 2 duck legs

Directions:

1. In a bowl, mix together the garlic, parsley, five-spice powder, salt and black pepper.
2. Rub the duck legs with garlic mixture generously.
3. Arrange the duck legs onto the greased sheet pan.
4. Press "Power Button" of Ninja Foodi Digital Air Fry Oven and turn the dial to select "Air Fry" mode.
5. Press "Time Button" and again turn the dial to set the cooking time to 30 minutes.
6. Now push "Temp Button" and rotate the dial to set the temperature at 340 degrees F.
7. Press "Start/Pause" button to start.
8. When the unit beeps to show that it is preheated, open the lid and insert the sheet pan in the oven.
9. Flip the duck legs once halfway through.
10. When cooking time is complete, open the lid and transfer the duck legs onto serving plates.
11. Serve hot.
12. Serving Suggestions: Serve these duck legs with cucmber salad.
13. Variation Tip: Never defrost the duck meat on the counter.

Air Fryer Chicken Wings

Servings: 4
Cooking Time: 30 Mins

Ingredients:

- 1-1/2 oz. chicken wings
- 1 tsp. garlic powder
- 1 tsp. kosher salt
- 1 tbsp. of butter, unsalted and melted
- ½ C. hot sauce

Directions:

1. Keep your chicken wings in 1 layer. Use paper towels to pat them dry.
2. Sprinkle garlic powder and salt evenly.
3. Now keep these wings in your air fryer at 380°F.
4. Cook for 20 minutes. Toss after every 5 minutes. The wings should be cooked through and tender.
5. Bring up the temperature to 400 degrees F.
6. Cook for 5-8 minutes until it has turned golden brown and crispy.
7. Toss your wings with melted butter (optional) before serving.

Olive-brined Turkey Breast

Servings: 14
Cooking Time: 20 Mins

Ingredients:

- 3-1/2 oz. turkey breasts, boneless and skinless
- ½ C. buttermilk
- ¾ C. olive brine
- 2 sprigs of thyme
- 1 rosemary sprig

Directions:

1. Bring together the buttermilk and olive brine.
2. Keep the turkey breast in a plastic bag. Pour the buttermilk-brine mix into this.
3. Add the thyme sprigs and rosemary.
4. Seal and bag. Keep it refrigerated.
5. Take it out after 8 hours. Set it aside and wait for it to reach room temperature.
6. Preheat your air fryer to 175 degrees C or 350 degrees F.
7. Cook the turkey breast for 12 minutes.
8. Flip over and cook for another 5 minutes. The turkey's center shouldn't be pink.

Bang-bang Chicken

Servings: 6
Cooking Time: 15 Mins

Ingredients:

- 1 oz. chicken breast tenderloins, small pieces
- ½ C. sweet chili sauce
- 1 C. of mayonnaise
- 1-1/2 C. bread crumbs
- 1/3 C. flour

Directions:

1. Whisk the sweet chili sauce and mayonnaise together in a bowl.
2. Spoon out 3 quarters of a C. from this. Set aside.
3. Keep flour in a plastic bag. Add the chicken and close this bag. Coat well by shaking.
4. Place the coated chicken in a large bowl with the mayonnaise mix.
5. Combine well by stirring.
6. Keep your bread crumbs in another plastic bag.
7. Place chicken pieces into the bread crumbs. Coat well.
8. Preheat your air fryer to 200 degrees C or 400 degrees F.
9. Transfer the chicken into the basket of your air fryer. Do not overcrowd.
10. Cook for 7 minutes.
11. Flip over and cook for another 4 minutes.
12. Transfer the chicken to a bowl. Pour over the reserved sauce.
13. You can also sprinkle some green onions before serving.

Lemony Turkey Legs

Servings: 2
Cooking Time: 30 Mins

Ingredients:

- 2 garlic cloves, minced
- 1 tbsp. fresh rosemary, minced
- 1 tsp. fresh lemon zest, finely grated
- 2 tbsp. olive oil
- 1 tbsp. fresh lemon juice
- Salt and freshly ground black pepper, to taste
- 2 turkey legs

Directions:

1. In a large bowl, mix together the garlic, rosemary, lime zest, oil, lime juice, salt, and black pepper.
2. Add the turkey legs and coat with marinade generously.
3. Refrigerate to marinate for about 6-8 hours.
4. Press "Power Button" of Ninja Foodi Digital Air Fry Oven and turn the dial to select "Air Fry" mode.
5. Press "Time Button" and again turn the dial to set the cooking time to 30 minutes.
6. Now push "Temp Button" and rotate the dial to set the temperature at 350 degrees F.
7. Press "Start/Pause" button to start.
8. When the unit beeps to show that it is preheated, open the lid and grease the air fry basket.
9. Arrange the turkey legs into the prepared basket and insert in the oven.
10. Flip the turkey legs once halfway through.
11. When cooking time is complete, open the lid and transfer the turkey legs onto serving plates.
12. Serve hot.
13. Serving Suggestions: Serve these turkey legs with honey macadamia stuffing.
14. Variation Tip: A fresh turkey meat should never be chilled below 26 degrees.

Spicy Chicken Legs

Servings: 6
Cooking Time: 25 Mins

Ingredients:

- 2½ lb. chicken legs
- 2 tbsp. olive oil
- 1 tsp. smoked paprika
- 1 tsp. garlic powder
- ½ tsp. ground cumin
- Salt and freshly ground black pepper, to taste

Directions:

1. In a large bowl, add all the ingredients and mix well.
2. Arrange the chicken legs onto a sheet pan.
3. Press "Power Button" of Ninja Foodi Digital Air Fry Oven and turn the dial to select "Air Fry" mode.
4. Press "Time Button" and again turn the dial to set the cooking time to 25 minutes.
5. Now push "Temp Button" and rotate the dial to set the temperature at 400 degrees F.
6. Press "Start/Pause" button to start.
7. When the unit beeps to show that it is preheated, open the lid and insert the sheet pan in the oven.
8. When cooking time is complete, open the lid and transfer the chicken legs onto serving plates.
9. Serve hot.
10. Serving Suggestions: Serve with cheesy baked asparagus.
11. Variation Tip: Don't accept any chicken legs that are soft and discolored.

Bacon-wrapped Chicken Breasts

Servings: 4
Cooking Time: 23 Mins

Ingredients:

- 1 tbsp. palm sugar
- 6-7 Fresh basil leaves
- 2 tbsp. fish sauce
- 2 tbsp. water
- 2 (8-ounces) chicken breasts, cut each breast in half horizontally
- Salt and freshly ground black pepper, to taste
- 12 bacon strips
- 1½ tsp. honey

Directions:

1. In a small heavy-bottomed pan, add palm sugar over medium-low heat and cook for about 2-3 minutes or until caramelized, stirring continuously.
2. Add the basil, fish sauce and water and stir to combine.
3. Remove from heat and transfer the sugar mixture into a large bowl.
4. Sprinkle each chicken breast with salt and black pepper.
5. Add the chicken pieces in the sugar mixture and coat generously.
6. Refrigerate to marinate for about 4-6 hours.
7. Wrap each chicken piece with 3 bacon strips.
8. Coat each piece with honey slightly.
9. Press "Power Button" of Ninja Foodi Digital Air Fry Oven and turn the dial to select "Air Fry" mode.
10. Press "Time Button" and again turn the dial to set the cooking time to 20 minutes.
11. Now push "Temp Button" and rotate the dial to set the temperature at 365 degrees F.
12. Press "Start/Pause" button to start.
13. When the unit beeps to show that it is preheated, open the lid and grease the air fry basket.
14. Arrange the chicken breasts into the prepared basket and insert in the oven.
15. Flip the chicken breasts once halfway through.
16. When cooking time is complete, open the lid and transfer the chicken breasts onto serving plates.
17. Serve hot.
18. Serving Suggestions: Serve with balsamic-glazed green beans.
19. Variation Tip: Use thick-cut bacon strips.

Seasoned Chicken Tenders

Servings: 2
Cooking Time: 10 Mins

Ingredients:

- 8 oz. chicken tenders
- 1 tsp. BBQ seasoning
- Salt and ground black pepper, as required

Directions:

1. Line the "Sheet Pan" with a lightly, greased piece of foil.
2. Set aside.
3. Season the chicken tenders with BBQ seasoning, salt and black pepper.
4. Arrange the chicken tenders onto the prepared "Sheet Pan" in a single layer.
5. Press "Power Button" of Ninja Foodi Digital Air Fry Oven and turn the dial to select the "Air Bake" mode.
6. Press the Time button and again turn the dial to set the cooking time to 10 minutes.
7. Now push the Temp button and rotate the dial to set the temperature at 450 degrees F.
8. Press "Start/Pause" button to start.
9. When the unit beeps to show that it is preheated, open the lid and insert "Sheet Pan" in the oven.
10. Serve hot.

Spiced Chicken Thighs

Servings: 4
Cooking Time: 20 Mins

Ingredients:
- 1 tsp. ground cumin
- 1 tsp. garlic powder
- ½ tsp. smoked paprika
- ½ tsp. ground coriander
- Salt and ground black pepper, as required
- 4 (5-oz.) chicken thighs

Directions:
1. In a large bowl, add the spices, salt and black pepper and mix well.
2. Coat the chicken thighs with oil and then rub with spice mixture.
3. Arrange the chicken thighs onto the sheet pan.
4. Press "Power Button" of Ninja Foodi Digital Air Fry Oven and turn the dial to select "Air Fry" mode.
5. Press "Time Button" and again turn the dial to set the cooking time to 20 minutes.
6. Now push "Temp Button" and rotate the dial to set the temperature at 400 degrees F.
7. Press "Start/Pause" button to start.
8. When the unit beeps to show that it is preheated, open the lid and insert the sheet pan in the oven.
9. Flip the chicken thighs once halfway through.
10. When cooking time is complete, open the lid and transfer the chicken thighs onto serving plates.
11. Serve hot.
12. Serving Suggestions: Serve with a fresh green salad.
13. Variation Tip: Adjust the ratio of spices according to your spice tolerance.

Asian Deviled Eggs

Servings: 12
Cooking Time: 15 Mins

Ingredients:
- 6 eggs
- 2 tbsp. of mayonnaise
- 1 tsp. soy sauce, low-sodium
- 1-1/2 tsp. of sesame oil
- 1 tsp. Dijon mustard

Directions:
1. Keep the eggs on the air fryer rack. Make sure that there is adequate space between them.
2. Set the temperature to 125 degrees C or 160 degrees F.
3. Air fry for 15 minutes.
4. Take out the eggs from your air fryer. Keep in an ice water bowl for 10 minutes.
5. Take them out of the water. Now peel and cut them in half.
6. Scoop out the yolks carefully. Keep in a food processor.
7. Add the sesame oil, mayonnaise, Dijon mustard, and soy sauce.
8. Process until everything combines well. The mixture should be creamy.
9. Fill up your piping bag with this yolk mixture. Distribute evenly into the egg whites. They should be heaping full.
10. You can garnish with green onions and sesame seeds (optional).

Glazed Chicken Drumsticks

Servings: 4
Cooking Time: 20 Mins

Ingredients:

- ¼ C. Dijon mustard
- 1 tbsp. maple syrup
- 2 tbsp. olive oil
- 1 tbsp. fresh rosemary, minced
- Salt and freshly ground black pepper, to taste
- 4 (6-oz.) chicken drumsticks

Directions:

1. In a bowl, add all ingredients except the drumsticks and mix until well combined.
2. Add the drumsticks and coat with the mixture generously.
3. Cover the bowl and refrigerate to marinate overnight.
4. Place the chicken drumsticks into the greased baking pan.
5. Press "Power Button" of Ninja Foodi Digital Air Fry Oven and turn the dial to select "Air Fry" mode.
6. Press "Time Button" and again turn the dial to set the cooking time to 12 minutes.
7. Now push "Temp Button" and rotate the dial to set the temperature at 320 degrees F.
8. Press "Start/Pause" button to start.
9. When the unit beeps to show that it is preheated, open the lid and insert baking pan in the oven.
10. After 12 minutes, flip the drumsticks and set the temperature to 390 degrees F for 8 minutes.
11. When cooking time is complete, open the lid and transfer the chicken drumsticks onto serving plates.
12. Serve hot.
13. Serving Suggestions:
14. Variation Tip: You can increase the quantity of maple syrup according to your taste.

Crispy Roasted Chicken

Servings: 7
Cooking Time: 40 Mins

Ingredients:

- 1 (3½-pound) whole chicken, cut into 8 pieces
- Salt and ground black pepper, as required
- 2 C. buttermilk
- 2 C. all-purpose flour
- 1 tbsp. ground mustard
- 1 tbsp. garlic powder
- 1 tbsp. onion powder
- 1 tbsp. paprika

Directions:

1. Rub the chicken pieces with salt and black pepper.
2. In a large bowl, add the chicken pieces and buttermilk and refrigerate to marinate for at least 1 hour.
3. Meanwhile, in a large bowl, place the flour, mustard, spices, salt and black pepper and mix well.
4. Grease the cooking racks generously.
5. Remove the chicken pieces from bowl and drip off the excess buttermilk.
6. Coat the chicken pieces with the flour mixture, shaking any excess off.
7. Press "Power Button" of Ninja Foodi Digital Air Fry Oven and turn the dial to select the "Air Fry" mode.
8. Press the Time button and again turn the dial to set the cooking time to 20 minutes.
9. Now push the Temp button and rotate the dial to set the temperature at 390 degrees F.
10. Press "Start/Pause" button to start.
11. When the unit beeps to show that it is preheated, open the lid and grease "Air Fry Basket".
12. Arrange half of the chicken pieces into "Air Fry Basket" and insert in the oven.
13. Repeat with the remaining chicken pieces.
14. Serve immediately.

Thyme Duck Breast

Servings: 2
Cooking Time: 20 Mins

Ingredients:

- 1 C. beer
- 1 tbsp. olive oil
- 1 tsp. mustard
- 1 tbsp. fresh thyme, chopped
- Salt and freshly ground black pepper, to taste
- 1 (10½-oz.) duck breast

Directions:

1. In a bowl, add the beer, oil, mustard, thyme, salt, and black pepper and mix well
2. Add the duck breast and coat with marinade generously.
3. Cover and refrigerate for about 4 hours.
4. Arrange the duck breast onto the greased sheet pan.
5. Press "Power Button" of Ninja Foodi Digital Air Fry Oven and turn the dial to select "Air Fry" mode.
6. Press "Time Button" and again turn the dial to set the cooking time to 20 minutes.
7. Now push "Temp Button" and rotate the dial to set the temperature at 390 degrees F.
8. Press "Start/Pause" button to start.
9. When the unit beeps to show that it is preheated, open the lid and insert the sheet pan in the oven.
10. Flip the duck breast once halfway through.
11. When cooking time is complete, open the lid and place the duck breast onto a cutting board for about 5 minutes before slicing.
12. With a sharp knife, cut the duck breast into desired size slices and serve.
13. Serving Suggestions: Duck meat goes really well with caramelized onions or balsamic reduction.
14. Variation Tip: Look for a plump, firm breast for best flav

Herbed & Spiced Turkey Breast

Servings: 6
Cooking Time: 40 Mins

Ingredients:

- ¼ C. butter, softened
- 2 tbsp. fresh rosemary, chopped
- 2 tbsp. fresh thyme, chopped
- 2 tbsp. fresh sage, chopped
- 2 tbsp. fresh parsley, chopped
- Salt and ground black pepper, as required
- 1 (4-pound) bone-in, skin-on turkey breast
- 2 tbsp. olive oil

Directions:

1. In a bowl, add the butter, herbs, salt and black pepper and mix well.
2. Rub the herb mixture under skin evenly.
3. Coat the outside of turkey breast with oil.
4. Place the turkey breast into the greased baking pan.
5. Press "Power Button" of Ninja Foodi Digital Air Fry Oven and turn the dial to select the "Air Bake" mode.
6. Press the Time button and again turn the dial to set the cooking time to 40 minutes.
7. Now push the Temp button and rotate the dial to set the temperature at 350 degrees F.
8. Press "Start/Pause" button to start.
9. When the unit beeps to show that it is preheated, open the lid and insert baking pan in the oven.
10. Remove from oven and place the turkey breast onto a platter for about 5-10 minutes before slicing.
11. With a sharp knife, cut the turkey breast into desired sized slices and serve.

Fish & Seafood Recipes

Zesty Fish Fillets

Servings: 4
Cooking Time: 12 Mins

Ingredients:

- 4 fillets of salmon or tilapia
- 2-1/2 tsp. vegetable oil
- ¾ C. crushed cornflakes or bread crumbs
- 2 eggs, beaten
- 1 packet dry dressing mix

Directions:

1. Preheat the air fryer to 180° C.
2. Mix the dressing mix and the breadcrumbs together.
3. Pour the oil. Stir until you see the mix getting crumbly and loose.
4. Now dip your fish fillets into the egg. Remove the excess.
5. Dip your fillets into the crumb mix. Coat evenly.
6. Transfer to the fryer carefully.
7. Cook for 10 minutes. Take out and serve.
8. You can also add some lemon wedges on your fish.

Crusted Salmon

Servings: 2
Cooking Time: 15 Mins

Ingredients:

- 2 (6-oz.) skinless salmon fillets
- Salt and ground black pepper, as required
- 3 tbsp. walnuts, chopped finely
- 3 tbsp. quick-cooking oats, crushed
- 2 tbsp. olive oil

Directions:

1. Rub the salmon fillets with salt and black pepper evenly.
2. In a bowl, mix together the walnuts, oats and oil.
3. Arrange the salmon fillets onto the greased "Sheet Pan" in a single layer.
4. Place the oat mixture over salmon fillets and gently, press down.
5. Press "Power Button" of Ninja Foodi Digital Air Fry Oven and turn the dial to select the "Air Bake" mode.
6. Press the Time button and again turn the dial to set the cooking time to 15 minutes.
7. Now push the Temp button and rotate the dial to set the temperature at 400 degrees F.
8. Press "Start/Pause" button to start.
9. When the unit beeps to show that it is preheated, open the lid.
10. Insert the "Sheet Pan" in oven.
11. Serve hot.

Tartar Sauce Fish Sticks

Servings: 4
Cooking Time: 15 Mins

Ingredients:
- 1 oz. fillets of cod, cut into small sticks
- ¾ C. mayonnaise
- 1-1/2 C. bread crumbs
- 2 tbsp. of dill pickle relish
- 1 tsp. seafood seasoning

Directions:
1. Combine the relish, seafood seasoning, and the mayonnaise in a bowl.
2. Include the fish. Stir gently to coat.
3. Preheat your air fryer to 200 degrees C or 400 degrees F.
4. Keep the bread crumbs on your plate.
5. Coat the sticks of fish in the crumbs one at a time.
6. Transfer the fish sticks to your air fryer basket. Place in one single layer. They shouldn't be touching each other.
7. Cook for 10 minutes.
8. Take out from the basket. Set aside for a minute.
9. Keep in a plate lined with a paper towel before serving.

Herbed Scallops

Servings: 2
Cooking Time: 14 Mins

Ingredients:

- ¾ lb. sea scallops, cleaned and pat dry
- 1 tbsp. butter, melted
- ¼ tbsp. fresh thyme, minced
- ¼ tbsp. fresh rosemary, minced
- Salt and freshly ground black pepper, to taste

Directions:

1. In a large bowl, place the scallops, butter, herbs, salt, and black pepper and toss to coat well.
2. Press "Power Button" of Ninja Foodi Digital Air Fry Oven and turn the dial to select "Air Fry" mode.
3. Press "Time Button" and again turn the dial to set the cooking time to 4 minutes.
4. Now push "Temp Button" and rotate the dial to set the temperature at 390 degrees F.
5. Press "Start/Pause" button to start.
6. When the unit beeps to show that it is preheated, open the lid and grease the air fry basket.
7. Arrange the scallops into the air fry basket and insert in the oven.
8. When cooking time is complete, open the lid and transfer the scallops onto serving plates.
9. Serve hot.
10. Serving Suggestions: Potato fries will be great with these scallops.
11. Variation Tip: Remove the side muscles from the scallops.

Crumbed Fish

Servings: 4
Cooking Time: 12 Mins

Ingredients:

- 4 flounder fillets
- 1 C. bread crumbs
- 1 egg, beaten
- ¼ C. of vegetable oil
- 1 lemon, sliced

Directions:

1. Preheat your air fryer to 180 degrees C or 350 degrees F.
2. Mix the oil and bread crumbs in a bowl. Keep stirring until you see this mixture becoming crumbly and loose.
3. Now dip your fish fillets into the egg. Remove any excess.
4. Dip your fillets into the bread crumb mix. Make sure to coat evenly.
5. Keep the coated fillets in your preheated fryer gently.
6. Cook until you see the fish flaking easily with a fork.
7. Add lemon slices for garnishing.

Cod Parcel

Servings: 2
Cooking Time: 15 Mins

Ingredients:

- 2 tbsp. butter, melted
- 1 tbsp. fresh lemon juice
- ½ tsp. dried tarragon
- Salt and freshly ground black pepper, to taste
- ½ C. red bell peppers, seeded and thinly sliced
- ½ C. carrots, peeled and julienned
- ½ C. fennel bulbs, julienned
- 2 (5-oz.) frozen cod fillets, thawed
- 1 tbsp. olive oil

Directions:

1. In a large bowl, mix together the butter, lemon juice, tarragon, salt, and black pepper.
2. Add the bell pepper, carrot, and fennel bulb and generously coat with the mixture.
3. Arrange 2 large parchment squares onto a smooth surface.
4. Coat the cod fillets with oil and then sprinkle evenly with salt and black pepper.
5. Arrange 1 cod fillet onto each parchment square and top each evenly with the vegetables.
6. Top with any remaining sauce from the bowl.
7. Fold the parchment paper and crimp the sides to secure fish and vegetables.
8. Press "Power Button" of Ninja Foodi Digital Air Fry Oven and turn the dial to select "Air Fry" mode.
9. Press "Time Button" and again turn the dial to set the cooking time to 15 minutes.
10. Now push "Temp Button" and rotate the dial to set the temperature at 350 degrees F.
11. Press "Start/Pause" button to start.
12. When the unit beeps to show that it is preheated, open the lid.
13. Arrange the cod parcels into the air fry basket and insert in the oven.
14. When cooking time is complete, open the lid and transfer the cod parcels onto serving plates.
15. Carefully open the parcels and serve hot.
16. Serving Suggestions: Serve with the drizzling of lime juice.
17. Variation Tip: You can use veggies of your choice.

Buttered Salmon

Servings: 2
Cooking Time: 10 Mins

Ingredients:

- 2 (6-oz.) salmon fillets
- Salt and freshly ground black pepper, to taste
- 1 tbsp. butter, melted

Directions:

1. Season each salmon fillet with salt and black pepper and then, coat with the butter.
2. Press "Power Button" of Ninja Foodi Digital Air Fry Oven and turn the dial to select "Air Fry" mode.
3. Press "Time Button" and again turn the dial to set the cooking time to 10 minutes.
4. Now push "Temp Button" and rotate the dial to set the temperature at 360 degrees F.
5. Press "Start/Pause" button to start.
6. When the unit beeps to show that it is preheated, open the lid and grease the air fry basket.
7. Arrange the salmon fillets into the prepared air fry basket and insert in the oven.
8. When cooking time is complete, open the lid and transfer the salmon fillets onto serving plates.
9. Serve hot.
10. Serving Suggestions: Enjoy with roasted parsnip puree.
11. Variation Tip: Salmon should look bright and shiny.

Spiced Tilapia

Servings: 2
Cooking Time: 12 Mins

Ingredients:

- ¼ tsp. garlic powder
- ¼ tsp. onion powder
- ¼ tsp. ground cumin
- Salt and ground black pepper, as required
- 2 (6-oz.) tilapia fillets
- 1 tbsp. butter, melted

Directions:

1. In a small bowl, mix together the spices, salt and black pepper.
2. Coat the tilapia fillets with oil and then rub with spice mixture.
3. Press "Power Button" of Ninja Foodi Digital Air Fry Oven and turn the dial to select the "Air Fry" mode.
4. Press the Time button and again turn the dial to set the cooking time to 12 minutes.
5. Now push the Temp button and rotate the dial to set the temperature at 360 degrees F.
6. Press "Start/Pause" button to start.
7. When the unit beeps to show that it is preheated, open the lid.
8. Arrange the tilapia fillets over the greased "Wire Rack" and insert in the oven.
9. Flip the tilapia fillets once halfway through.
10. Serve hot.

Herbed Salmon

Servings: 2
Cooking Time: 10 Mins

Ingredients:

- 1 tbsp. fresh lime juice
- ½ tbsp. olive oil
- Salt and freshly ground black pepper, to taste
- 1 garlic clove, minced
- ½ tsp. fresh thyme leaves, chopped
- ½ tsp. fresh rosemary, chopped
- 2 (7-oz.) salmon fillets

Directions:

1. In a bowl, add all the ingredients except the salmon and mix well.
2. Add the salmon fillets and coat with the mixture generously.
3. Press "Power Button" of Ninja Foodi Digital Air Fry Oven and turn the dial to select "Air Bake" mode.
4. Press "Time Button" and again turn the dial to set the cooking time to 10 minutes.
5. Now push "Temp Button" and rotate the dial to set the temperature at 400 degrees F.
6. Press "Start/Pause" button to start.
7. When the unit beeps to show that it is preheated, open the lid.
8. Arrange the salmon fillets over the greased wire rack and insert in the oven.
9. Flip the fillets once halfway through.
10. When cooking time is complete, open the lid and transfer the salmon fillets onto serving plates.
11. Serve hot.
12. Serving Suggestions: Serve with steamed asparagus.
13. Variation Tip: For best result, use freshly squeezed lime juice.

Ranch Tilapia

Servings: 4
Cooking Time: 13 Mins

Ingredients:

- ¾ C. cornflakes, crushed
- 1 (1-oz.) packet dry ranch-style dressing mix
- 2½ tbsp. vegetable oil
- 2 eggs
- 4 (6-oz.) tilapia fillets

Directions:

1. In a shallow bowl, crack the eggs and beat slightly.
2. In another bowl, add the cornflakes, ranch dressing, and oil and mix until a crumbly mixture forms.
3. Dip the fish fillets into egg and then, coat with the bread crumbs mixture.
4. Press "Power Button" of Ninja Foodi Digital Air Fry Oven and turn the dial to select "Air Fry" mode.
5. Press "Time Button" and again turn the dial to set the cooking time to 13 minutes.
6. Now push "Temp Button" and rotate the dial to set the temperature at 356 degrees F.
7. Press "Start/Pause" button to start.
8. When the unit beeps to show that it is preheated, open the lid and grease the air fry basket.
9. Arrange the tilapia fillets into the prepared air fry basket and insert in the oven. When cooking time is complete, open the lid and transfer the fillets onto serving plates.
10. Serve hot.
11. Serving Suggestions: Serve tilapia with lemon butter.
12. Variation Tip: The skin should be removed, either before cooking or before serving.

Lobster Tails with Garlic Butter-lemon

Servings: 2
Cooking Time: 10 Mins

Ingredients:

- 2 lobster tails
- 1 tsp. lemon zest
- 4 tbsp. of butter
- 1 garlic clove, grated
- 2 wedges of lemon

Directions:

1. Butterfly the lobster tails. Use kitchen shears to cut by length through the top shell's center and the meat.
2. Cut to the bottom portion of the shells.
3. Now spread halves of the tail apart.
4. Keep these tails in the basket of your air fry. The lobster meat should face up.
5. Melt the butter in your saucepan.
6. Add the garlic and lemon zest. Heat for 30 seconds.
7. Transfer two tbsp. of this mix to a bowl.
8. Brush on your lobster tails. Remove the remaining brushed butter.
9. Season with pepper and salt.
10. Cook in your air fryer at 195 degrees C or 380 degrees F. The lobster meat should turn opaque in about 5 or 7 minutes.
11. Apply the reserved butter over the lobster meat.
12. You can serve with lemon wedges.

Buttered Trout

Servings: 2
Cooking Time: 10 Mins

Ingredients:

- 2 (6-ounces) trout fillets
- Salt and ground black pepper, as required
- 1 tbsp. butter, melted

Directions:

1. Season each trout fillet with salt and black pepper and then, coat with the butter.
2. Arrange the trout fillets onto the greased "Sheet Pan" in a single layer.
3. Press "Power Button" of Ninja Foodi Digital Air Fry Oven and turn the dial to select the "Air Fry" mode.
4. Press the Time button and again turn the dial to set the cooking time to 10 minutes.
5. Now push the Temp button and rotate the dial to set the temperature at 360 degrees F.
6. Press "Start/Pause" button to start.
7. When the unit beeps to show that it is preheated, open the lid.
8. Insert the "Sheet Pan" in oven.
9. Flip the fillets once halfway through.
10. Serve hot.

Lemon Dill Mahi Mahi

Servings: 2
Cooking Time: 15 Mins

Ingredients:

- 2 fillets of Mahi Mahi, thawed
- 2 lemon slices
- 1 tbsp. olive oil
- 1 tbsp. lemon juice
- 1 tbsp. dill, chopped

Directions:

1. Combine the olive oil and lemon juice in a bowl. Stir.
2. Keep the fish fillets on a parchment paper sheet.
3. Brush the lemon juice mix on each side. Coat heavily.
4. Season with pepper and salt.
5. Add the chopped dill on top.
6. Keep the fillets of Mahi Mahi in your air fryer basket.
7. Cook at 400° F for 12 minutes.
8. Take out. Serve immediately.

Prawn Burgers

Servings: 2
Cooking Time: 6 Mins

Ingredients:

- ½ C. prawns, peeled, deveined and chopped very finely
- ½ C. breadcrumbs
- 2-3 tbsp. onion, chopped finely
- ½ tsp. fresh ginger, minced
- ½ tsp. garlic, minced
- ½ tsp. red chili powder
- ½ tsp. ground cumin
- ¼ tsp. ground turmeric
- Salt and freshly ground black pepper, to taste

Directions:

1. In a bowl, add all ingredients and mix until well combined.
2. Make small sized patties from mixture.
3. Press "Power Button" of Ninja Foodi Digital Air Fry Oven and turn the dial to select "Air Fry" mode.
4. Press "Time Button" and again turn the dial to set the cooking time to 6 minutes.
5. Now push "Temp Button" and rotate the dial to set the temperature at 355 degrees F.
6. Press "Start/Pause" button to start.
7. When the unit beeps to show that it is preheated, open the lid and grease the air fry basket.
8. Arrange the patties into the prepared air fry basket and insert in the oven.
9. When cooking time is complete, open the lid and transfer the burgers onto serving plates.
10. Serve hot.
11. Serving Suggestions: Serve with tomato ketchup.
12. Variation Tip: Don't use frozen shrimp in this recipe.

Glazed Salmon

Servings: 2
Cooking Time: 8 Mins

Ingredients:

- 2 (6-oz.) salmon fillets
- Salt, to taste
- 2 tbsp. honey

Directions:

1. Sprinkle the salmon fillets with salt and then coat with honey.
2. Press "Power Button" of Ninja Foodi Digital Air Fry Oven and turn the dial to select "Air Fry" mode.
3. Press "Time Button" and again turn the dial to set the cooking time to 8 minutes.
4. Now push "Temp Button" and rotate the dial to set the temperature at 355 degrees F.
5. Press "Start/Pause" button to start.
6. When the unit beeps to show that it is preheated, open the lid and grease the air fry basket.
7. Arrange the salmon fillets into the prepared air fry basket and insert in the oven.
8. When cooking time is complete, open the lid and transfer the salmon fillets onto serving plates.
9. Serve hot.
10. Serving Suggestions: Fresh baby greens will be great if served with glazed salmon.
11. Variation Tip: honey can be replaced with maple syrup too.

Vegetarian And Vegan Recipes

Basil Tomatoes

Servings: 2
Cooking Time: 10 Mins

Ingredients:

- 3 tomatoes, halved
- Olive oil cooking spray
- Salt and freshly ground black pepper, to taste
- 1 tbsp. fresh basil, chopped

Directions:

1. Drizzle the cut sides of the tomato halves with cooking spray evenly.
2. Then, sprinkle with salt, black pepper and basil.
3. Press "Power Button" of Ninja Foodi Digital Air Fry Oven and turn the dial to select "Air Fry" mode.
4. Press "Time Button" and again turn the dial to set the cooking time to 10 minutes.
5. Now push "Temp Button" and rotate the dial to set the temperature at 320 degrees F.
6. Press "Start/Pause" button to start.
7. When the unit beeps to show that it is preheated, open the lid.
8. Arrange the tomatoes into the air fry basket and insert in the oven.
9. When cooking time is complete, open the lid and transfer the tomatoes onto serving plates.
10. Serve warm.
11. Serving Suggestions: You can use these tomatoes in pasta and pasta salads with a drizzle of balsamic vinegar.
12. Variation Tip: Fresh thyme can also be used instead of basil.

Garlicky Brussels Sprout

Servings: 4
Cooking Time: 15 Mins

Ingredients:

- 1 lb. Brussels sprouts, cut in half
- 2 tbsp. oil
- 2 garlic cloves, minced
- ¼ tsp. red pepper flakes, crushed
- Salt and freshly ground black pepper, to taste

Directions:

1. In a bowl, add all the ingredients and toss to coat well.
2. Press "Power Button" of Ninja Foodi Digital Air Fry Oven and turn the dial to select "Air Fry" mode.
3. Press "Time Button" and again turn the dial to set the cooking time to 12 minutes.
4. Now push "Temp Button" and rotate the dial to set the temperature at 390 degrees F.
5. Press "Start/Pause" button to start.
6. When the unit beeps to show that it is preheated, open the lid.
7. Arrange the Brussels sprouts into the air fry basket and insert in the oven.
8. When cooking time is complete, open the lid and transfer the Brussels sprouts onto serving plates.
9. Serve hot.
10. Serving Suggestions: Sprinkle with flaky sea salt before serving.
11. Variation Tip: Look for small to medium sprouts for better taste.

Roasted Cauliflower and Broccoli

Servings: 6
Cooking Time: 15 Mins

Ingredients:

- 3 C. cauliflower florets
- 3 C. of broccoli florets
- ¼ tsp. of sea salt
- ½ tsp. of garlic powder
- 2 tbsp. olive oil

Directions:

1. Preheat your air fryer to 200 degrees C or 400 degrees F.
2. Keep your florets of broccoli in a microwave-safe bowl.
3. Cook in your microwave for 3 minutes on high temperature. Drain off the accumulated liquid.
4. Now add the olive oil, cauliflower, sea salt, and garlic powder to the broccoli in the bowl.
5. Combine well by mixing.
6. Pour this mix now into your air fryer basket.
7. Cook for 10 minutes. Toss the vegetables after 5 minutes for even browning.

Parmesan Asparagus

Servings: 3
Cooking Time: 10 Mins

Ingredients:

- 1 lb. fresh asparagus, trimmed
- 1 tbsp. Parmesan cheese, grated
- 1 tbsp. butter, melted
- 1 tsp. garlic powder
- Salt and freshly ground black pepper, to taste

Directions:

1. In a bowl, mix together the asparagus, cheese, butter, garlic powder, salt, and black pepper.
2. Press "Power Button" of Ninja Foodi Digital Air Fry Oven and turn the dial to select "Air Fry" mode.
3. Press "Time Button" and again turn the dial to set the cooking time to 10 minutes.
4. Now push "Temp Button" and rotate the dial to set the temperature at 400 degrees F.
5. Press "Start/Pause" button to start.
6. When the unit beeps to show that it is preheated, open the lid and grease the air fry basket.
7. Arrange the veggie mixture into the prepared air fry basket and insert in the oven.
8. When cooking time is complete, open the lid and transfer the asparagus onto serving plates.
9. Serve hot.
10. Serving Suggestions: Serve with the garnishing of pine nuts.
11. Variation Tip: you can use fresh garlic instead of garlic powder.

Fried Green Tomatoes

Servings: 6
Cooking Time: 20 Mins

Ingredients:

- 2 tomatoes, cut into small slices
- ½ C. buttermilk
- 2 eggs, beaten lightly
- 1 C. bread crumbs
- 1/3 C. of all-purpose flour
- 1 C. yellow cornmeal

Directions:

1. Season the slices of tomato with pepper and salt.
2. Take 2 breeding dishes. Keep flour in the first, stir in eggs and buttermilk in the second, and mix cornmeal and bread crumbs in the third.
3. Dredge the slices of tomato in your flour. Shake off any excess.
4. Now dip the tomatoes in the egg mix.
5. Then dip into the bread crumb mix. Coat both sides.
6. Preheat your air fryer to 200 degrees C or 400 degrees F.
7. Brush olive oil on the fryer basket.
8. Keep the slices of tomato in your fryer basket. They shouldn't touch.
9. Brush some olive oil on the tomato tops.
10. Cook for 10 minutes. Flip your tomatoes, brush olive oil and cook for another 5 minutes.
11. Take the tomatoes out. Keep in a rack lined with a paper towel.

Potato Tots

Servings: 24
Cooking Time: 35 Mins

Ingredients:

- 2 peeled sweet potatoes
- Olive oil cooking spray
- ½ tsp. Cajun seasoning
- Sea salt to taste

Directions:

1. Boil a pot of water. Add the sweet potatoes in it.
2. Keep boiling until you can pierce them using a fork.
3. It should take about 15 minutes. Don't over boil, as they can get too messy for grating. Drain off the liquid. Allow it to cool.
4. Grate the potatoes in a bowl.
5. Now mix your Cajun seasoning carefully.
6. Create tot-shaped cylinders with this mixture.
7. Spray some olive oil on your fryer basket.
8. Keep the tots in it. They should be in 1 row and shouldn't be touching each other or the basket's sides.
9. Apply some olive oil spray on the tots.
10. Heat your air fryer to 200 degrees C or 400 degrees F.
11. Cook for 8 minutes.
12. Flip over and cook for 8 more minutes after applying the olive oil spray again.

Broccoli With Cauliflower

Servings: 6
Cooking Time: 15 Mins

Ingredients:

- 1-pound broccoli, cut into 1-inch florets
- 1-pound cauliflower, cut into 1-inch florets
- 2 tbsp. butter
- Salt and ground black pepper, as required
- ¼ C. Parmesan cheese, grated

Directions:

1. In a pan of the boiling water, add the broccoli and cook for about 3-4 minutes.
2. Drain the broccoli well.
3. In a bowl, place the broccoli, cauliflower, oil, salt, and black pepper and toss to coat well.
4. Press "Power Button" of Ninja Foodi Digital Air Fry Oven and turn the dial to select the "Air Fry" mode.
5. Press the Time button and again turn the dial to set the cooking time to 15 minutes.
6. Now push the Temp button and rotate the dial to set the temperature at 400 degrees F.
7. Press "Start/Pause" button to start.
8. When the unit beeps to show that it is preheated, open the lid.
9. Arrange the veggie mixture in "Air Fry Basket" and insert in the oven.
10. Toss the veggie mixture once halfway through.
11. Remove from oven and transfer the veggie mixture into a large bowl.
12. Immediately, stir in the cheese and serve immediately.

Sweet & Tangy Mushrooms

Servings: 4
Cooking Time: 15 Mins

Ingredients:

- ¼ C. soy sauce
- ¼ C. honey
- ¼ C. balsamic vinegar
- 2 garlic cloves, chopped finely
- ½ tsp. red pepper flakes, crushed
- 18 oz. cremini mushrooms, halved

Directions:

1. In a bowl, place the soy sauce, honey, vinegar, garlic and red pepper flakes and mix well. Set aside.
2. Place the mushroom into the greased baking pan in a single layer.
3. Press "Power Button" of Ninja Foodi Digital Air Fry Oven and turn the dial to select the "Air Bake" mode.
4. Press the Time button and again turn the dial to set the cooking time to 15 minutes.
5. Now push the Temp button and rotate the dial to set the temperature at 350 degrees F.
6. Press "Start/Pause" button to start.
7. When the unit beeps to show that it is preheated, open the lid.
8. Insert the baking pan in oven.
9. After 8 minutes of cooking, place the honey mixture in baking pan and toss to coat well.
10. Serve hot.

Corn Nuts

Servings: 8
Cooking Time: 25 Mins

Ingredients:

- 1 oz. white corn
- 1-1/2 tsp. salt
- 3 tbsp. of vegetable oil

Directions:

1. Keep the corn in a bowl. Cover this with water. Keep aside for 8 hours minimum for hydration.
2. Drain the corn. Spread it on a baking sheet. They should be in an even layer.
3. Use paper towels to pat dry. Also air dry for 15 minutes.
4. Preheat your air fryer to 200 degrees C or 400 degrees F.
5. Transfer the corn to a bowl. Add salt and oil. Stir to coat evenly.
6. Keep the corn in your air fryer basket in an even layer.
7. Cook for 8 minutes.
8. Shake the basket and cook for 8 minutes more.
9. Shake the basket once more. Cook for 5 more minutes.
10. Transfer to a plate lined with a paper towel.
11. Set aside for allowing the corn nuts to cool. They should be crisp.

Sweet Potato Hash

Servings: 6
Cooking Time: 15 Mins

Ingredients:

- 2 sweet potatoes, cubed into small pieces
- 2 tbsp. of olive oil
- 1 tsp. black pepper, ground
- 1 tbsp. of smoked paprika
- 1 tsp. dill weed, dried

Directions:

1. Preheat your air fryer to 200 degrees C or 400 degrees F.
2. Toss the olive oil, sweet potatoes, paprika, pepper, and salt in a bowl.
3. Keep this mixture in your air fryer.
4. Now cook for 12 minutes.
5. Check first, and then stir after 8 minutes. Stir after another 2 minutes. It should turn brown and crispy.

Stuffed Zucchini

Servings: 4
Cooking Time: 35 Mins

Ingredients:

- 2 zucchinis, cut in half lengthwise
- ½ tsp. garlic powder
- Salt, as required
- 1 tsp. olive oil
- 4 oz. fresh mushrooms, chopped
- 4 oz. carrots, peeled and shredded
- 3 oz. onion, chopped
- 4 oz. goat cheese, crumbled
- 12 fresh basil leaves
- ½ tsp. onion powder

Directions:

1. Carefully, scoop the flesh from the middle of each zucchini half.
2. Season each zucchini half with a little garlic powder and salt.
3. Arrange the zucchini halves into the greased baking pan.
4. Place the oat mixture over salmon fillets and gently, press down.
5. Press "Power Button" of Ninja Foodi Digital Air Fry Oven and turn the dial to select the "Air Bake" mode.
6. Press the Time button and again turn the dial to set the cooking time to 20 minutes.
7. Now push the Temp button and rotate the dial to set the temperature at 450 degrees F.
8. Press "Start/Pause" button to start.
9. When the unit beeps to show that it is preheated, open the lid.
10. Insert the baking pan in oven.
11. Meanwhile, in a skillet, heat the oil over medium heat and cook the mushrooms, carrots, onions, onion powder and salt and cook for about 5-6 minutes.
12. Remove from the heat and set aside.
13. Remove the baking pan from oven and set aside.
14. Stuff each zucchini half with veggie mixture and top with basil leaves, followed by the cheese.
15. Press "Power Button" of Ninja Foodi Digital Air Fry Oven and turn the dial to select the "Air Bake" mode.
16. Press the Time button and again turn the dial to set the cooking time to 15 minutes.
17. Now push the Temp button and rotate the dial to set the temperature at 450 degrees F.
18. Press "Start/Pause" button to start.
19. When the unit beeps to show that it is preheated, open the lid.
20. Insert the baking pan in oven.

Buttered Veggies

Servings: 3
Cooking Time: 20 Mins

Ingredients:

- 1 C. potatoes, chopped
- 1 C. beets, peeled and chopped
- 1 C. carrots, peeled and chopped
- 2 garlic cloves, minced
- Salt and ground black pepper, as required
- 3 tbsp. olive oil

Directions:

1. In a bowl, place all ingredients and toss to coat well.
2. Place the tofu mixture in the greased "Sheet Pan".
3. Press "Power Button" of Ninja Foodi Digital Air Fry Oven and turn the dial to select the "Air Bake" mode.
4. Press the Time button and again turn the dial to set the cooking time to 20 minutes.
5. Now push the Temp button and rotate the dial to set the temperature at 450 degrees F.
6. Press "Start/Pause" button to start.
7. When the unit beeps to show that it is preheated, open the lid.
8. Insert the "Sheet Pan" in oven.
9. Toss the veggie mixture once halfway through.
10. Serve hot.

Roasted Vegetables

Servings: 4
Cooking Time: 20 Mins

Ingredients:

- 1 yellow squash, cut into small pieces
- 1 red bell pepper, seeded and cut into small pieces
- ¼ oz. mushrooms, cleaned and halved
- 1 tbsp. of extra-virgin olive oil
- 1 zucchini, cut into small pieces

Directions:

1. Preheat your air fryer. Keep the squash, red bell pepper, and mushrooms in a bowl.
2. Add the black pepper, salt, and olive oil. Combine well by tossing.
3. Keep the vegetables in your fryer basket.
4. Air fry them for 15 minutes. They should get roasted. Stir about halfway into the roasting time.

Fried Chickpeas

Servings: 4
Cooking Time: 20 Mins

Ingredients:
- 1 can chickpeas, rinsed and drained
- 1 tbsp. olive oil
- 1 tbsp. of nutritional yeast
- 1 tsp. garlic, granulated
- 1 tsp. of smoked paprika

Directions:
1. Spread the chickpeas on paper towels. Cover using a second paper towel later.
2. Allow them to dry for half an hour.
3. Preheat your air fryer to 180 degrees C or 355 degrees F.
4. Bring together the nutritional yeast, chickpeas, smoked paprika, olive oil, salt, and garlic in a mid-sized bowl. Coat well by tossing.
5. Now add your chickpeas to the fryer.
6. Cook for 16 minutes until they turn crispy. Shake them in 4-minute intervals.

Roasted Okra

Servings: 1
Cooking Time: 15 Mins

Ingredients:

- ½ oz. okra, trimmed ends and sliced pods
- ¼ tsp. salt
- 1 tsp. olive oil
- 1/8 tsp. black pepper, ground

Directions:

1. Preheat your air fryer to 175 degrees C or 350 degrees F.
2. Bring together the olive oil, okra, pepper, and salt in a mid-sized bowl.
3. Stir gently.
4. Keep in your air fryer basket. It should be in one single layer.
5. Cook for 5 minutes in the fryer. Toss once and cook for another 5 minutes.
6. Toss once more. Cook again for 2 minutes.

Lightning Source UK Ltd.
Milton Keynes UK
UKHW052102300123
416186UK00012B/438